Ezekiel's Wheel Within A Wheel

by
David Mathews

CCB Publishing
British Columbia, Canada

Ezekiel's Wheel Within A Wheel

Copyright ©2020 by David Mathews
ISBN-13   978-1-77143-425-6
First Edition

Library and Archives Canada Cataloguing in Publication
Title: Ezekiel's wheel within a wheel / by David Mathews.
Names: Mathews, David, 1958- author.
Description: First edition.
Identifiers: Canadiana (print) 2020028827X | Canadiana (ebook) 20200288555 |
ISBN 9781771434256 (softcover) | ISBN 9781771434263 (PDF)
Subjects: LCSH: Bible. Ezekiel—Criticism, interpretation, etc. |
LCSH: Bible. Old Testament—Criticism, interpretation, etc.
Classification: LCC BS1545.52 .M38 2020 | DDC 224/.406—dc23

All Scriptural quotes are from the 1987 version of the KJV Bible and are in the Public Domain.

All other authors' quotes or materials written or otherwise contained herein are quoted by permission and/or are in the Public Domain.

All images contained herein are reproduced by permission from the copyright holder or are in the Public Domain.

Cover artwork credit: © Simon Wong
Email: simon-wong@live.co.uk / Website: www.simon-wong.co.uk

The Hebrew fonts contained within are from BibleWorks.
"BWHEBB, BWHEBL, BWTRANSH [Hebrew]; BWGRKL, BWGRKN, and BWGRKI [Greek] PostScript® Type 1 and TrueType fonts Copyright ©1994-2013 BibleWorks, LLC. All rights reserved. These Biblical Greek and Hebrew fonts are used with permission and are from BibleWorks (www.bibleworks.com).

Extreme care has been taken by the author to ensure that all information presented in this book is accurate and up to date at the time of publishing. Neither the author nor the publisher can be held responsible for any errors or omissions. Additionally, neither is any liability assumed for damages resulting from the use of the information contained herein.

All rights reserved. No part of this publication may be reproduced, stored in a retrieval system or transmitted in any form or by any means, electronic, mechanical, photocopying, recording or otherwise without the express written permission of the author, except in the case of excerpts used in brief reviews or publications.

For information regarding written permission or for author interviews please contact:
Manna from Heaven Ministries
7488 Mt. Angel Hwy NE
Silverton, OR 97381
www.livingmanna.net

Publisher: CCB Publishing
                British Columbia, Canada
                www.ccbpublishing.com

Dedication

To my wife, Brenda:

Thank you once again for your patience as we walked the vision of this book out together!

Acknowledgements

The list here is special: Our House has endured much in the pursuit of our King! It doesn't look the same as it did arriving in Oregon 8 years ago! However, the heart and soul of those who stood with me throughout has been revealed numerous times! To the Manna Crew: Your faithfulness is awesome! Thank you Brenda, Brittney, Joy, B. J., Brandy, and Daniel: Alongside them – The House of Flores and Remnant of Truth International who joined their strength with ours. Pastor John, I salute you and Rochelle!

Lastly, I want to honor Simon Wong for his kindness in allowing the use of his artwork for the cover page!

https://www.facebook.com/simonwongart

Disclaimer

The research into this work is exhaustive and a compilation of a decade of prayer and thousands of hours spent digging into the Language of the Creator to extract the revelation found beneath the depths. Though some may have bits and pieces of the content found within I have taken great pains to ensure that no other work has been copied, no collusion sought with other teachers or authors. There were simply none to be found treating this subject from the vantage point allowed us by the Ruach HaKodesh – The Set Apart Spirit! I stand humbled before Him!

What you will find within is a breathtaking headfirst dive into the Vision of Ezekiel that will change forever how you view the subjects contained inside these covers!

David Mathews

Books by David Mathews

The Rainbow Language:
The Sight, Sound & Color of the Holy Tongue
Published 2015 – ISBN 9781771432399

The Serpent's Seed:
They're Among Us
Published 2016 – ISBN 9781771432856

Ezekiel's Wheel Within A Wheel
Published 2020 – ISBN 9781771434256

Contents

Foreword ix
Preface xi

Chapter 1:   Ezekiel's Wheel in the Middle of A Wheel 1

Chapter 2:   Familiar Faces? 14

Chapter 3:   The Heavenly Prophetic Pattern
             and Genesis 3 27

Chapter 4:   The Tabernacle – The Man Inside the
             Wheel Within the Wheel 40

Chapter 5:   Enoch: The Genuine and the Counterfeit! 53

Chapter 6:   Not Convinced of A Divine Connection? 63

Chapter 7:   Where is Eden Today? Does it Exist? 78

Chapter 8:   A Closer Look into the Breastplate Stones
             Worn by This Heylel Being… 92

Chapter 9:   The Hidden Keys: Alef & Tav! 109

Chapter 10: Three Calendars? 360-364-365 Which
             One Do We Use? 123

Chapter 11: Ezekiel's Tabernacle and the Bones of
             Redemption: Ezekiel 37:1-28 139

Foreword

"It is the Glory of Elohiym to conceal a matter and it is the honor of His royal ones to bring to surface that which was concealed." (John-James amplified version of this verse found in Proverbs 25:2) Over the years I have been mentored by several, embraced by many and gleaned from the wisdom of such men and women that have changed my life and have helped my spiritual walk with our Abba who is in Heaven. These principles have overflowed into my personal life as a believer, a husband, a father and now a grandfather. I have had the honor and privilege to come across the path of another man of honor, mentor and spiritual father in my life that I have been able to learn from and glean vital life skills and tools of ministry that has kept me to this day as well as some of the deepest revelations of scripture I have ever heard. Having said this, I would like to share for a moment what I deem an important thought.

This compelling masterpiece, in my personal opinion, is one that is not to be taken lightly. The Library of scrolls as seen in the Book of Ezekiel is one of compelling and riveting discussion that has pierced through the pages of time. The Book or Library of Ezekiel I truly believe and am convinced holds keys to end time prophecy and current events that have come upon the doorstep of this generation. Many questions have not found a home regarding this revelation of Ezekiel's wheels, until now. Imagine what was going through the mind of the Prophet Ezekiel at this moment with such a demonstrative event that would grab the hand of eternity and the hand of what would be a distant future and cause that to be tangible and life changing. Ezekiel stood at the place where cycles, wheels, the most powerful angelic beings of which we still can't capture and who spoke from the highest places of Heaven and the most sacred corridors of the inner Chambers of The Great and Dreadful Presence revealed by The Wheel Within the Wheel.

Pastor David Mathews of Manna from Heaven Ministries has been on the cutting edge of prophecy and revelation of things pertaining to the Hebrew language and revelations you and I would only see captured in movies to a small degree. Pastor David Mathews the great author of two masterpieces so far, *The Rainbow Language: The Sight, Sound & Color of the Holy Tongue* and *The Serpent's Seed: They're Among Us* has now come with the crown of his labor, *Ezekiel's Wheel Within A Wheel*. I can't wait to read and see the picture he has painted of this ancient revelation that speaks of the days we have come to now and the near future our hands have been placed upon. I am already captivated and on the edge of my seat, who would like to come and join me as we all open the pages of *Ezekiel's Wheel Within A Wheel* and discover some of the most riveting and deepest revelations come to life before our eyes? Let us begin to take a part in this honor by searching out this revelation we now have at our fingertips.

Shalom Aleichem
Shepherd John-James Remnant of Truth International

Preface

Dear Reader:

We are about to embark on a monumental journey. One that will test your resolve and qualify your perspective of what Truth is versus what you've held as such and historically viewed through the lens of your traditional religious interpretation. You will embrace this work or trash it. There can be no middle ground. It is simply too abrasive and challenging. Why? Every Believer has formed some opinion of the End Times and most find any scholarly threat to that opinion as an opportunity to disengage from discussion. I have found few who were established on a foundation sure enough that when presented with a divergent view could openly embrace a suddenly revealed Truth!

That being said, the contents of this book will stretch you and though it may seem indigestible to begin with, it is my prayer that the sheer volume of evidence will lend itself as the tool found prying you off that stump of stubbornness that so often keeps us from enjoying the freedom that comes from seeing reality as it was meant to be!

We will examine every major theme addressed in this book and we will test it against the only truly authentic certainty: The Language of Creation itself – Hebrew! No other language, regardless of interpretation, no transliteration irrespective of the credentialed scholar who may offer it, is sufficient in this regard.

This way, if an argument ensues we cannot offer a contrary opinion unless we can agree on a case law that is capable of settling our differences. That Case Law must be the Hebrew Language of the Scriptures for nothing else will suffice!

Armed with the above the Vision of Ezekiel and the myriads of interwoven connections to the Past, Present and the Future and those ancient sign posts of Noah's Ark, the Wilderness Tabernacle, the Tabernacle of King David, their design construct and how it relates to the ancient Stellar Signs of the Zodiac and much more – will release their long hidden secrets and you will never be the same!

I pray that you will diligently seek Him throughout and that you will commit to rightly dividing the Word of Truth. If so, the Plans that He has for you are about to take a sharp, hard turn and your destiny is just around that corner! Embrace it! Delight yourself in Him and He will give you the desires of your heart!

Please know that we are here for you. Our contact information is provided and we will be accessible to discuss any concerns you may encounter! Are you ready? Then let's… Unleash The Hounds!

David Mathews

Chapter 1

Ezekiel's Wheel in the Middle of A Wheel

We are about to embark on a grand journey you and I! We will travel places in the Scriptures that have long been abandoned by Main Stream Believers, simply because it is too exhaustive to think outside the box when simple traditions will suffice. If you are willing, we will be stretched beyond our comfort zone and I promise you, we will find proof – evidence buried below a millennium of subterfuge and obfuscation that will explode your understanding of where we are currently and where we're headed in the future on the Prophetic Calendar of the Creator of the Universe! Are you ready? If so, fasten your seatbelts and let's ride!

For almost 8 years this passage from which we've taken our book title has resonated in my spirit. I've spent hours looking at the enigmatic revelations buried within its verses and I'm convinced those hidden revelations are keys to unlocking the mysteries of the above mentioned Calendar, the coming Tabernacle of David, and the synchronization of the Holy Convocations – all, in order that they fit properly in their respective places in what we flippantly call End-Time Prophecy and much more!

However my dear Reader, finding our way through the layers of traditional misinterpretations (Deliberate and otherwise) is like traversing a maze with a blindfold! To the initiate there seems no

Ezekiel's Wheel Within A Wheel

logical way out! Though our task is daunting, amid the Centuries of blatant contradiction and compromise there are answers and frankly, they are awaiting the disciples of truth. Ours is not an assignment for the faint hearted or the lazy man; Therefore, I must ask before you waste your time reading further – are you willing to go there?

I assume (If you're still reading) that you are hungry for His Truth and indeed as I write this, many of you are handpicked by Abba to form the most powerful entity ever known – The Body of Messiah! Armed with this information in mind, and coupled with the fact that Ezekiel is considered a benchmark for end-time prophetic discussion, join me as we dare to attempt to unravel the mysteries, and expose the contradictions. Not only is it possible, I promise you will see things few have ever seen! Let's get down to business, shall we?

Though the initial focus of the title is on the 'Beings' described as attending the "Vehicle or Wheel within a wheel," we must backtrack a bit earlier in the scroll to an innocuous statement found in Ezekiel 2:9 which quite clearly reveals an agenda given these 'Beings'. One, in practical terms, whose true purpose is in reality, to deliver to the Prophet a *roll of a book. [Sic KJV]* The Hebrew actually says: "A megillot Sepher": What makes this obscure phrase important? Let's examine these two words in their Hebrew context.

- Roll: H#4039 *#1   מגלת   *Megillot*

    The Hebrew letter Mem as a prefix indicates from or out of, the origin or source of something, it pictures the Womb the source of all beginnings. This Mem refers us to the 3-letter root stem taken from Gimmel-Lamed-Hey, galah. This root forms words indicating: to reveal,

---

* #1. Note: All Strong's Exhaustive concordance Hebrew numbers will be listed in this fashion: H#4039

uncover, to expose, as well as, exile and/or captivity. The original meaning of galah as found in several key places is one of rolling, to roll onto or to commit trust to someone!

- Book: H#5612   ספר   *Sepher*

This becomes a letter of instruction, a document, or deed, and to serve an indictment, show the evidence, and simply, a scroll. Further, as a verb it infers to etch or score with a mark, to inscribe! The individual letters Samech-Pey-Resh, hint at supporting or sustaining something as in a Remnant, the Par or fruit, the Seed out of the rebellious House of Israel!

Since the root of megillot means a roll or circle we're not stretching things to assert the possibility of it reflecting a cyclical, future generational influence on those "End-Times". Additionally, it is entirely plausible from the above definitions to deduce that Ezekiel is being shown a future generation, though an exiled, hidden Remnant, which will be born out of the womb of this book! Did you catch that? Doesn't that sound eerily similar to the Outcasts of Israel who will be gathered according to ancient Prophecy?

Immediately, from this perspective, we can surmise that the singular purpose of this Visit of these 'Beings' is first to reveal the plan of YHVH in rolling away the future captivity of His people – *if they will trust Him* – by the plan written in the Scroll now being shown to Ezekiel! Indeed! It is also possible for us to gain a much broader perspective from the deeper meanings of the above words, as it seems the intention of those plans is namely: That they are to be hidden for a season, until those same TRUSTED ONES arrive!

In all honesty dear Reader, we have a mandate to rightly divide the Truth (2 Tim. 2:15). Take a look at the sayings of the Wise Man found here in Proverbs. 25:2 *#2:

> *It is the glory of God to conceal a thing: but the honour-kavod of kings is to search out a matter!*

That being said, the Hebrew language is an alphanumeric tongue. Each letter serving as both a numeral and a letter! *#3 When this is considered the possibility that both numbers and their Letter equivalent can be found supporting one another, as factual evidence testifying of Truth, it should induce our labor and begin the birthing of Revelation!

By way of illustration, not only will their identity be unveiled – but also the specific timeframe, future meeting place(s), and perhaps even a Wilderness like itinerary of 42 stages or rendezvous points where protection, sanctuary, sustenance, and instruction awaits those who understand! This seems consistent with the 42 months of Megas Thlipsis or Great Tribulation spoken of throughout the Brit Chadashah or New Testament! Many Believers shy away from questioning Scripture, or their teachers or pastors for that matter, being content to swallow the "status quo" of ignorance that is most often guised in the cloak of tradition!

Let me show you a quick sample in support of our position thus far. If one counts the number of Hebrew letters in Ezekiel 2:9 above, which is 32, we find its numeric value the same as the gematria or numeric value of the word Kavod or glory seen above.

Subsequently, this understanding serves to prompt a further

---

* #2. Note: All Scriptural quotes are from the KJ Bible, 1987 version and are in the Public Domain.
* #3. Note: The first Hebrew letter Aleph and their respective number values Alef =1, Bet =2, Gimmel =3 and so on…

searching for the buried treasures similar to those found in Job 3:23 which says: *a man whose way is hidden does not know how to escape calamities...* In suggesting this, long winded though I've been, what I'm effectively doing is asking you, perhaps provoking you, dear Reader, by way of these hidden treasures, to consider the following question.

Is it possible that Ezekiel is initially showing us, in this first chapter, an enigma that has escaped the understanding of scholars for centuries and in truth, a prophetic revelation far more than what these Spiritual Beings are traditionally assumed doing – an act most often described as attending the *"wheel within a wheel"*? Further, could this be an enigma – the solving of which enhances our understanding exponentially more than the mere delivering of a "simple scroll"? In fact, could there be found hiding here the answer to an ancient puzzle revealing a future blueprint? Perhaps containing the details in which, Abba will preserve the Future Remnant? If so, what is their connection to the Scroll or Book and what is its purpose? It isn't surprising that the Cover-up begins at this very incident!

First, before we set the stage, for further confirmation, let's examine the author of this book referred to as Ezekiel. Interestingly, we have almost universal consensus that Ezekiel's Hebrew name is formed from a compound of two Hebrew words: Both of which are quite familiar to the biblical student – Chazak and El, literally defined as meaning: The Strength of Elohiym. Be that as it may, here Ezekiel is said to be the son of Buzi, H#941, בוזי, which the translators have defined as "My Shame or Contempt". The two names are contradictory and in my opinion, this defies Hebrew logic since Buzi has the same root stem: Bet-Zayin – as Boaz – meaning the Strong One Who Comes and as such, Buzi, could be rendered "my Strong One" from which we could see the natural reason for continuing the pattern found in his naming his son Ezekiel – The Strength of Elohiym!

Further, the mysterious incident of Ezekiel's encounter with the

"Living Creatures" occurs at a specific location: 'by the Chebar River'. נהר כבר transliterated as Nahar-Chebar. River here is nahar: The plain meaning one of a light or beam, that burns, shines or flows, while the Hebrew word Chebar: Kaf-Bet-Resh, indicates a length of space or continuance of time, to augment or add to a quantity or number by binding them together (*Could this be a collection of dates/a calendar?*).

To simplify for those not familiar with Hebrew, Chebar means "ALREADY" – in the sense of future events that derive from ancient patterns long established. In essence, a future date in which something determined has already happened! Incidentally, the same Hebrew letters of Chebar rearranged to form Bet-Kaf-Resh can also indicate Bechor – Firstborn! Perhaps, with your permission, thus being excused for my excitement, we will share the hidden truth in this passage.

What is hidden you ask (As we plumb the depths of the Hebrew language which are fathomless) frankly, it is in this mental frenzy I find myself considering and thus, seeing far more than just the textual approbation! Can you see it? Oh my! Dear Reader – The truth is, it appears as if time is suspended while these Living Creatures are in the same dimension as Ezekiel! To support this position, Isaiah says:

> *Declaring the end from the beginning, and from ancient times the things that are not yet done, saying, My counsel shall stand, and I will do all my pleasure.* Isaiah 46:10

Compelling though my theory may be, while untested, on its merits, the fact remains here in Ezekiel 3:14 that he does in all actuality, seem to have been *"translated" physically* by these Living Creatures in order to deliver a specific message to his brethren in captivity. Was this the only purpose of these Beings? Is it possible that the Hebrew language of the Tanak reveals their mode of dimensional travel as conceivably the method by which dissemination of the future message will also transpire? What?

Am I suggesting a dimensional portal, a gateway, perhaps time travel? We seem to forget that our Creator is the answer to impossible possibilities! For that matter, Ezekiel, is in good company if this is indeed feasible! Why? Because Enoch experienced this portal, as did Moshe, Elijah, Yahshua, as well as, Paul, and Phillip the Evangelist!

Moreover, as we dissect each of the definitions mentioned above it seems there's a hidden reference again to the potential recipient of this future Prophetic Message; The One referred to as the Strong One, the Light Who Burns, the First Born Who Comes at a future date! Once again we find substance in the joint confirmation found in the numbers where the combined numeric Value of both Nahar and Chebar, equals 477, the exact same gematria as the phrase את היונה, the ET-h'yonah, the Alef-Tav or Sign of Jonah! The very sign that became legal parlance of those connecting both Yahshua as Messiah and the House of Israel, who would serve as a future Messiah figure linked dually as well, to this symbol!

As we reiterate, it seems diagnosing the encounter in the following manner, reveals it wholly as an enigma, perplexing; yet, a cryptic encounter unreservedly designed to reveal to Ezekiel and those of us from the future with an ear to hear, a prophetic picture of the future Redemption and Restoration of Israel as the Firstborn of YHVH and possibly, even more incredibly – *the timing for this event!* So, without hesitation we must investigate the ancient images known to have belonged to these Living Creatures…

The Faces of a Man-Lion-Ox-Eagle

I've taken the liberty of assuming you're already familiar with the vivid descriptions given these Creatures. What I will do for you here in order to expedite understanding is point you backward in antiquity to other remarks that unquestionably confirm their identity. The stunning depiction of these "creatures" via the KJV translators here in Ezekiel has prohibited most from connecting the dots with the aforementioned other places and events! Nevertheless, a detailed analysis of those previous details will lend remarkable clues of their identity and perchance their motives. Perhaps a furtive: *Have we seen them before* whisper is forming?

To be candid, in deference to the scholarly among us, these "faces" should initially remind us of the symbols attached to 4 of the Standards of the 12 Tribes of Israel, specifically their camping alignment around the Tabernacle. It is noteworthy that the camping alignment is different from the birth order of these same tribes. In addition, doubtless every Reader will stipulate that the Tabernacle was given to Moshe in a pattern after the similitude of the heavenlies. Admittedly, it is my opinion that the Tabernacle itself represented the central hub, the Throne or dwelling place of YHVH on the earth, much like the heavenly Throne, surrounded by the celestial bodies. Astoundingly similar to how we find this Wheel surrounded by these Celestial Creatures. This is another *Marker Code* giving validity to what we will find revealed as we pursue the Truth! In a nutshell, each "Face" as a Standard or ordinal point, is associated with the tribal camping alignment, and seems to also represent a compass point within a circle rather than a square or rectangular one! Before we proceed, remember that the compass is depicted as a 360 degree Circle! Each quadrant representing 90 degrees of the circle!

Perhaps we've been trying for 3500 years to fit the proverbial 'square-peg' in a round hole! To wit, a round or cyclical compass should require a round camping alignment that would encircle a round tabernacle! If such is the case, conventional views of a rectangular Tabernacle may not be correct! LET THAT SINK IN!

Pausing here for a second, I must say in passing, the Tabernacle was most often called the *Tent of the Congregation*, not Tent of

Meeting as most assume, the Hebrew phrase being אֹהֶל מוֹעֵד ohel mo'ed. This word mo'ed is almost always connected or defined by its first usage in Gen. 1:14 where it is found describing the set times or calendar of YHVH. Why then, would the translators render this word 'meeting' instead of more aptly using the aforementioned Tent of the Congregation or mo'ed which is easily rendered – *Tent of YHVH's Calendar or Set Times?*

Perchance we may have stumbled upon a clue that will explode the paradigm of traditional thinking regarding this 'Tabernacle Pattern'? Is it plausible, in a manner of speaking to consider the design of the Tent as one divinely inspired device whose dimensions contain a living calendar with incremental stages allowing for the determination of exact dates, time, and even Global Positioning? Hmmm? Why weren't the Children of Israel ever really 'lost' in their Wilderness excursion? Come to think of it, who would orchestrate a campaign to hide the facts of a Circular Tent designed for such a purpose? Can you say 'conspiracy theorist'?

Oh, where's my validation you ask? I would never presume you'd want otherwise! By chance, did you notice that the gematria of the phrase ohel mo'ed is 156, the same as that of Yoceph or Joseph and curiously, Ezekiel! Amazingly, it is the tribe of Joseph – (Depicted in his sons Ephraim and Manasseh) – whose standard stood to the west of the Tabernacle and within whose territory the Tent of the Congregation (Also known as, the Tent of David, *which, is wholeheartedly ignored by the Eschatological Interpreters of our future and which, is surely going to be restored bringing Unity to the House of Israel, an achievement not gained in the building of a 3rd Temple*) would have stood! I know! Incredulity rules the day here! But, stay with me, stay with me! We will give a preponderance of evidence before we're finished!

Let's take a breath and we'll come back to this but first let's visit the 'Standards' as they're listed: The Man, Lion, Ox and Eagle.

- The Man: H#120   אדם   ʾAdam

    This sign is associated with the Tribe of Reuben whose name is traditionally rendered – 'Behold a Son': His tribe would have been situated to the south. With him also were Simeon – translated as 'Hear' and Gad – normally rendered as 'Troop'. A deeper look reveals that Gad actually comes from a root meaning something painful or troublesome, an invasive cut into something in order to reveal a treasure. This would naturally follow the pattern of the first Adam who had invasive surgery in order to reveal his wife – Ishah, who would later be called Eve – Chavah! Both would live in the inter-dimensional time warp of Eden. It was here, that the first Tent of Appointed Times stood transcending both physical and spiritual worlds! The Man depicted here in the heavenly Circle or Zodiacal archetype of which the Tabernacle is said to be a pattern, is universally known as Aquarius, The Water-Bearer, who would have occupied the 6:00 or southern position.

- The Lion: H#738   ארי   ʾAriy

    Belonging to the Tribe of Judah, a name most often defined as praise, this sign is oriented to the east. Though the word can also infer a 'lion', the root stem hints at a violent plucking or gathering, to cast, viz. to reap! It is also cognate with words indicating a flaming altar, a holocaust! Accompanying Judah – To cast, to stand in front of – and Praise were Issachar – He brings a recompense, and Zebulon – To endow, bestow or glorify! Its heavenly sign is that of Leo and would occupy the eastern most or 3:00 position. Next in progression is…

- Ox: H#7794 שׁוֹר *Showr*

Most often presented is Taurus as the sign or banner belonging the House of Joseph, expressly related to Ephraim who is found situated to the west in the tribal coalition along with Manasseh and Benjamin. The word Showr is defined here as 'Ox', yet it strangely enough, hints at: To turn, go round or about, to journey, notably for traffic or merchandize! It is quite alluringly related to the Hebrew word H#7891, shiyr – to sing! Causing us to wonder out loud of Joseph's future partial role as the Priesthood of Singers! *(Would the House of Joseph become the Praise and Worshippers of our day as well as, the one responsible for teaching Torah to the Nations?)* This celestial sign of Taurus sits at 9 o'clock oriented to the West! Next in our arrangement around the Tent is the…

- Eagle: H#5404 נֶשֶׁר *Nesher*

The Hebrew word nesher is an unused root meaning to lacerate. This banner represented true North. The wider extent of this word actually indicates a vulture instead of the eagle! This is rather a curious turn of events, as it augurs an ominous future when linked with the unfortunate images of the other 3 houses in this Decan: They are Dan, meaning 'to judge'; his is the emblem of the serpent an ill-fated omen forever menacing in its role. Following, is Asher, which is somewhat innocuously defined as 'happy'. Interestingly enough the root comes from the verb 'ashar' to go forward, straight, to set something right. The final tribe is Naphtali, a name haplessly recorded as 'wrestling'. A better understanding comes as we examine the root stem 'patal' that means to intentionally Twist or to be crafty, cunning. The Eagle is not seen as the sign here, rather, it has morphed into what is known as Scorpio. This constellation resides at the 12 o'clock position.

These latter 3 houses – Dan, Asher and Naphtali, of the elliptical zodiac represent the last 3 dark months, the 10th, 11th and 12th of the Hebrew calendar. It seems a premonition prophesying of dark consequences rides on the inference of their names, presaging a future day when their specific "Times" – in other words, their place or seasons or months represented by the faces of the eternal clock will be cunningly twisted, though once judged as correct, it will be set aright!

Could this oracular umbilical cord link us to the apocalyptic text of Dan. 7:25 where it is recorded the Anti-Messiah will think to change times and laws? Curiously, the Aramaic word used for time and times, is H#5732, עדן, iddan, rendered here as 'time', a year. The root is said to be from Strong's number H#5708, iddah. A powerful omen connected to the 'monthly menstrual or appointed time' of the female.

Upon closer scrutiny it is seen related to the Ayin-Vav-Dalet root indicating to duplicate, repeat, to testify, to turn back or return! The connection to Daniel above cannot be overstated! It is the considered opinion of this author that Daniel, Esther-Hadassah (Star-Hidden) and our Ezekiel were all contemporaries, surreptitiously involved in massaging the ancient Hebrew letters into their current Chaldean counterparts obfuscating for 2000 years the Language of Creation! This in effect cloaked the Eschatological Future in a shroud of confusion until the rebirth of the Pure Language of Zephaniah 3:9!

Further, bear in mind, this is the same Ayin-Dalet-Nun root as found in EDEN – The Garden of Appointed Times – the original location of the Tabernacle or dwelling place of YHVH! It was in Eden where the first menstrual flow occurred, a prophetic indicator of the death of the SEED and the renewal of Life! The very purpose of the shadow pictures depicted by the Living

Creatures and their 4 Cardinal points which reflect the menstrual and ovulational cycles of the female – Bride. Does the future bear for us, this same foreboding potential of exile outside the Garden of Appointed Times unless we decipher this code?

We will come back and visit this tribal alignment later…

Chapter 2

Familiar Faces?

Previous to our getting sidetracked a bit with a description of the Living Beings and how their counterparts among the Zodiacal Signs depict a remarkable House of Israel connection, we found exhaustive evidence of These 'Signs' both biblical and extra-biblical which lend, in our opinion, irrefutable confirmation linking the Living Beings, and their - Zodiacal Signs with each of the 4 Banner Tribes-Houses (Joseph-Ephraim, Reuben, Judah, Dan) and in particular their tribal alignment, and tribal affiliation.

In passing we have also discussed the possibility of their having been seen in other remote scriptural locations where the relatively poor KJV translation succeeded in obscuring their identification. The thought of this is exceptional to put it mildly and a conspiratorial provocation at the minimum! Mayhap, as we consider those "Other places" where these "Creatures" are seen the Reader will also conclude that these ignored texts when properly translated, reveal a contestable description of what has been traditionally accepted– and *one not of a new class of Angelic Hosts*! Rather, when prudence is applied the description confines itself to a class of Beings called 'Seraphim' an example of which, can be found both in Revelation 4:7, 8 and Isaiah 6:2. Here, a vivid narrative describes the Living Beings as each having a face and six wings and in the former, one full of eyes. Again, our conspiratorial flags begin waving when we find their portrayal, chronicled in the above, intentionally modified so as to be vastly different from that of King James' corrupted description found in Ezekiel 1:6,11! How dare I say this you ask? Look for yourself!

> *And every one had four faces, and every one had four wings. Thus were their faces: and their wings were stretched upward; two wings of every one were joined one to another, and two covered their bodies.*

וְאַרְבָּעָה פָנִים לְאֶחָת וְאַרְבַּע כְּנָפַיִם לְאַחַת לָהֶם

The Hebrew transliteration is as follows: Ve arba'ah Paniym le achat ve arba kanaphiym le achat lacham: This verse should read: *And each of the four had a face and each of the four had wings*! Paniym is often viewed a plural word yet can be translated both 'face and faces'. Consequently, context should help translators determine which! In this case they were not consistent! How? As stated, Paniym H#6440 פנים, is generally translated as face, and comes from the root 'panah' to turn; as in evening turning into morning, a passage of time. It comes from the 2-letter stem of Pey-Nun, pan, a corner, indicating an angle, which simply put, is when two lines converge at a shared point. A definition, which by its very nature, points to these 'Faces', as seen aligned at cardinal angles around the Tabernacle, and the *Wheel within the Wheel* whose hub or core becomes the center point at which other angles meet! Conversely, the 4-Faces describe 90-degree angles extending outward to the edge of the 360-degree circle much like a 12, 3, 6, 9 clock face! This is interesting because the 3, 6, 9 numerals are said to be the key to life! Is it a stretch to see these Faces at these same numeric intervals on the heavenly clock? 12-3-6-9?

As an aside, these numbers are also connected to the ancient Solfeggio musical frequencies that heal, deliver, etc.! Please note: 12 tribes, 12 months of 30 days = a 360 day calendar or solar procession, while the length in years for the Zodiacal procession is 2160 years! 2160/360 = 6! Man's tenure on earth is approximately 6,000 years x 360 = 2,160,000! Man's days are numbered at 120 [**Note Gen. 6:3] 120x3=360. 120 x 50 =6000. The diameter of the moon is almost 2160 miles. It does seem, in view of these numerical connections that these Creatures are also, somehow linked to a Cyclical Calendar of 360 days, each day representing 1-degree in the Sun's precession.

Further, though vividly described in several places, only Isaiah specifically names them in Isaiah 6:2 H#8314, שְׂרָפִים, calling them seraphim - from saraph, translated as serpent only in the sense of its fiery, poisonous bite. More literally, it indicates to burn quickly, wholly. Thus, these beings are the "Burning Ones"! Isn't it therefore plausible that if they indeed represent a Zodiacal fixture, that they function much like a Burning Lamp or Beacon calling attention to the specifics of their location? It is no stretch to connect these "Burning Lamps" to Genesis 15:5 where YHVH had previously taken Abram outside his tent.

**Note the word Tent in connection with THE TENT - as in Tent of Appointed Times:

> *And he brought him forth abroad, and said, Look now toward heaven, and tell the stars, if thou be able to number them: and he said unto him, So shall thy seed be.*

Earlier, Abram had stated that he had only his steward Eliezer of Damascus as an heir. Is it possible that we've misunderstood what was actually being said? Was Abram complaining or was he, in point of fact, reminding The Creator of the Covenant? The word for steward and Damascus come from the same root! Mem-Shin-Qof, Masaq! Therefore, the verse reads: I am childless and the steward-Masaq of my house is Eliezer of Damascus-Masaq: El-Ezer – translated, El is my Help who hails from Masaq? Steward is also Masaq H#4943, משק, Son of possession; did you catch that? *The verse could literally be translated! Eliezer - EL*

MY HELP- The Son of Possession - is – The Son of Possession or The Heir of My House! Abram seems to be prophetically declaring the very Covenant concerning which YHVH has taken Abram outside and is now pointing to, the eternal message that the Ancients knew to be written in The Stars! Recounting that message The Creator blatantly tells Abram to look – Nabat, to regard intently, and then to *Count – Saphar*, read, cipher, take account of the message in the stars!

Coincidentally [Sarcasm mine ☺] this chapter is where Abram is recorded offering a sacrifice, and afterward is put to sleep while a SMOKING FURNACE AND A *BURNING LAMP* passes between the pieces! This same Burning Lamp Person is seen in our study text in Ezekiel 1:13! He – The Living Lamp or Menorah is always seen when a HOUSE is being formed! [Example: Mt. Sinai is seen as being on fire amid the thunderings].

It continues intriguing me as I consider the Hebrew letters used above: The combination of Shin-Resh-Pey, saraph, are such that, when rearranged to form Shin-Pey-Resh they give us the root of H#8236, שִׁפְרָה, Shiphrah, a Hebrew word defined as brightness, to glisten, to shine forth as dawn – Shiphrah, in passing, was also the name of one of the Midwives of Israel in Exodus 1:15-22:

These women were called prophetically Shiphrah and Puah, (The latter trans. Splendid mouth or speech) further, it is because of their faithfulness in bringing forth the Son(s) of Israel with bright, shining speech, instead of allowing Pharaoh to kill them, that they are rewarded as stated in the text: *Elohiym made them houses!* Much like their Zodiacal counterparts above – The Seraphim Houses!

**Note: See Psalms 19:1-6 describing their Message and Heavenly Circuit, another connection to these Living Creatures depicted in the Circular Zodiacal heavens! Let's move on! Whew! Talk about unconventional thinking!

Though our study clearly revolves (Pun Intended) around the "Faces of the Creatures", we cannot fathom their true import without looking at the Tabernacle design.

**Note Exodus 25:9, 40 and Hebrews 8:5.

These texts validate our contention that this earthly Tabernacle design seems to have been modeled after the heavenly pattern, H#8403, תבנית, tavniyth. Tavniyth is an interesting choice of Hebrew words: *Rendered Pattern here, it is elsewhere translated as likeness, form, similitude and figure!*

The root stem comes from H#1129, בנה, banah, to begin to build, repair, as in a family name, a house. The Bet-Nun-Yod stem Beni, means 'My Son'. Thus, it seems likely this 'Pattern' was to be in the similitude or form of His Son! We have established in numerous other teachings that the Tabernacle was designed in the Form of a Man – However, what exactly was this form? Again, the mere idea of the pattern of This Tabernacle Man Image or form - somehow being literally 'fleshed' out in the Body of the United House of Israel and further, having the audacity to suggest it was in a congruent fashion with the construction of a generational house of Worship known as 'The Tabernacle of His Presence' and now impudently suggesting it may be affiliated with the Vision of Ezekiel's Wheel Within A Wheel is indeed, enough to set on edge the teeth of Rabbinic Scholars!

In view of the centuries of scholarly consideration I simply cannot fathom why this perspective has not been forthcoming on a larger scale! Perhaps it is simply the timing of the Creator? Nonetheless, the box of tradition has been formed, trapping within its rigid walls almost all scholars, who, upon hearing our views rush to nurture back to life their "professional" opinions, huffing and puffing as they breathe into the nostrils of that bigoted body of Clergymen forever standing in the hallowed halls of the Church!

Candidly, dear Reader, our willful ignorance in spite of the facts being unveiled, becomes the status quo monument to their unchallenged dogma! Amazing! Who would have believed the furor we've created in opposing tradition? All in support of their conventional rectangular construction of the Tabernacle and a Cross-Like alignment of the Tribes around it and so many other Sacred Cows of religion!

Be that as it may, Ezekiel's Wheel within a Wheel - with the Faces of the Creatures, their Connection respective to individual, specific Tribes and their assigned Month - each of which is itself related to a specific Constellational House within the Canopy or Circle of the Heavens makes it much more likely that the established square or rectangular Tribal camping alignment would have instead resembled more the face of a clock (A circle through which the Sun traverses in a Circuit, H#8622, תקופה, pronounced tequwphah, a circuit, revolution, a turning, as in a course of time) which, again all points to a much simpler circular pattern and are thus, as such, plainly not random! Hard to digest you say? Well let's put it a bit more straightforward: Why have we traditionally accepted a rectangular Tabernacle within a Circular alignment, a proverbial "Square peg in a round hole" when there are 360 degrees in a circle? Has there been an intentional effort to hide the true Tabernacle construction? Note this cryptic Talmudic statement. *#4 Then revisit our naïve attempt to glean truth from Scripture!

I hear you! You're willing to embrace newfound revelation only you want to see proof! I get that. 2nd Timothy 2:15 admonishes us to: *Study to show ourselves approved, workmen that need not be*

---

* #4. Talmudic Prohibitions: There are many sources citing the commentaries of ancient Sages such as Abaye, who taught that Torah expressly forbade the making of images of Temple furnishings, and further, a man could not make a house in the form of the Temple, its court, halls, etc. Note: See Rosh Hashanah 24b for additional info.

ashamed, by rightly dividing the word of truth! So, we will provide you with the materials, notes, textural interpretations and you rightly divide it, and then let's compare positions once we're finished! Agreed? Here are some to consider! I promise they will make you clean your palate of the leftover taste of your religious GMO's – genetically modified opinions!

Ancient Origins:
The Circle Around the Man:

Most theologians agree that the first 3 chapters of Genesis are rife with Temple language: This seems to inculcate the foundational principle known, as the "Law of First Reference". (The idea being that the first mention of a subject, sets a precedent of sorts regarding its future use) Since no one questions this Creational ideal as part of the original "temple pattern" why hasn't the specific form or design construct of the Tabernacle been searched as thoroughly?

Frankly, the coming 3rd Temple and how it affects the Believing community will become the most divisive subject ever to assault the minds and souls of those who are prisoners to the designs of an enemy who embodies himself as an angel of light! Thus, the Temple as a heavenly paragon cannot be overemphasized! We must challenge traditional concepts lest we fall prey to the delusional counterfeits that are sure to be a part of our prophetic future! And challenge we will! It is therefore fitting that we look at the beginning, B'reshiyt, the Book of Beginnings…

Please take note of Genesis 2:8:

> *And the LORD God planted a garden eastward in Eden; and there he put the man whom he had formed.*

The Hebrew word for garden found here is H#1588, גן, gan -

taken from ganan meaning to surround, to enclose. This is followed by the Hebrew word giving specific direction translated in the KJV as 'eastward' is H#6924, קדם, qadam, to be in front, precede, that which was before! The language concludes that Eden was a larger landmass that included gan Eden, the *garden in Eden*. Let me state it another way: Eden proper literally had the *Garden of Appointed Times, as its central hub!* Hold that thought and we'll clarify things a bit for you.

If we look back at the Hebrew word for planted, H#5193, נטע, nata', indicating to set upright, to establish, to plant, fix, to strike; we find it also having cognate roots which hint at assigning a fixed position. By uncloaking the mundane KJV English interpretation and taking a look at the more picturesque Hebrew word for 'planted' we find an homogeneous element eerily akin to a drummer marking a beat or cadence, to a fixed time! Stepping even further out on the limb here, it unquestionably sounds as if by placing him in the garden, that YHVH encircled the Man with *time in fixed degrees or increments* from the beginning of his original creation! Therefore, Man became a sort of 'Sun/Son Dial' charged with 'dressing and keeping' וּלְשָׁמְרָהּ לְעָבְדָהּ *le'avadah uleshamarah* – to work, labor, and serve, to execute, and to bring to pass. In other words - to accomplish the will of the Creator in incremental, step-by-step portions assigned a fixed incremental timeframe!

By breaking it down even further, *The Ayin-Dalet root of Avad, hints at a 'progression of time'* - this is particularly notable, because it implies, as part of his role in the Garden, that Adam was charged with guarding, observing, and watching, preserving something in order to keep it within bounds, in other words, he would mark its progression!

This is not an incidental assignment! There must have been a specific device, a mechanism or entity from which a cadence or beat emanated! Because in every respect Adam was a CLOCK WATCHER! Moreover, we believe that device to have been ingenuously established in the Heavens as detailed in Genesis 1:14 where the stellar luminaries are said to regulate day, night, years and seasons as well as, the Moedim or Holy Days! Such that, vividly describing a previously hidden role of Adam we observe he was undoubtedly charged with marking the progression of time both in the heavenly Zodiac above, and in Gan Eden synchronizing those marks by celebrating the Holy Convocations, the earthly pattern of time in the Garden where Messiah would routinely appear!

This 'theory' is staggeringly exciting because it begins to connect other threads of proof, indeed perhaps lending a credible nod towards our hypothesis of a Cyclical or Round Tabernacle! Yet, without a tenable purpose, Adam's merely serving as a 'Timekeeper' would have no foreseeable, feasible objective. Doubtless, the true design of the Creational Calendar has faded into religious oblivion, though it should be the lynchpin of every relationship! Why?

Why! Excuse my shouting at such religious incredulity! Dear Reader! Surely you can't argue the blatant, irreverent disregard by mainstream Christianity of a fixed, immutable calendar, where a SEVENTH-DAY SABBATH was clearly established in anticipation of a divine encounter between the Manifest Presence of the Creator and His Bride? He, who's eternal, design was to intentionally, romantically reveal Himself in all His Magnificence at those specific seasons! Let me show you inarguable evidence that has been suppressed by most; in particular, those professing themselves Biblical Scholars, rarely venturing a peek outside their religious blinders! Indignant am I, perhaps a tad impertinent? Take a look with me here at Genesis 3:8 and then come back and answer that! It is here where even the eviscerated KJV distinctly translates an Entity appearing and, His being referred to as, *'The Voice'* – He who Came Walking in the Cool of the Day…the Hebrew word for cool is Ruach, H#7307, רוח, spirit, wind, and breath. However, it also hints at a quarter, or quadrant, a point of the compass of heaven! At the moment of the Genesis 3 encounter Adam and Chavah – Eve were at the location known as belonging to the Tree of The Knowledge of Good and Evil, and the Tree of Life, both of which would have been situated NORTH in the Garden! How so? From whence is the throne of YHVH? The following are but two verses whose textural compass, points to the location of the above Throne.

> *Beautiful for situation, the joy of the whole earth, is mount Zion, on the sides of the north, the city of the great King.* Isaiah 14:13; *For thou hast said in thine heart, I will ascend into heaven, I will exalt my throne above the stars of God: I will sit also upon the mount of the congregation, in the sides of the north.* Psalms 48:2

Thus, Gan Eden (For those of you free-thinkers who enjoy stretching your mind beyond the conventional paradigm) can be seen as the place of the VOICE'S embarkation, since He has not been 'seen' until this specified time (Cool of the day) and could very well have been a dimensional, time-traveling portal between Heaven and Earth – A Ladder ascending and descending perhaps? By way of remembrance, we can conceivably connect the future dream and vision of Jacob's ladder here as well! Presumably, this was an established place and time where Yahshua, a.k.a. 'The Voice' would arrive in order to meet Adam and Chavah at the place of His earthly throne!

As monumental as this revelation is, juxtaposed to our chosen vehicle of travel here in Ezekiel – The Wheel Within a Wheel – it is reasonable to assume the conventional boundaries of time as we know it today would not have constrained Adam and Chavah, who most likely would have had access to inter-dimensional travel at thought-like speed upon or within this same conveyance!

Additionally, this place, this vehicle, the cyclical nature of the patterns of time, the charge given to Adam regarding the Gan Eden - are all part of the medium of transport whereby we find the subliminal message of Redemption forever blueprinted both in the Spirit realm and the Natural realm and are seen typecast in the Zodiacal blueprint, the Master Plan of the heavenlies!

Let me call your attention to Psalm 19:1-6:

> *The heavens declare the glory of God; and the firmament sheweth his handywork. Day unto day uttereth speech, and night unto night sheweth knowledge. There is no speech nor language, where their voice is not heard. Their line is gone out through all the earth, and their words to the end of the world. In them hath he set a tabernacle for the sun, Which is as a bridegroom coming out of his chamber, and rejoiceth as a strong man to run a race. His going forth is from the end of the heaven, and his circuit unto the ends of it: and there is nothing hid from the heat thereof.*

From this, and several other texts we can surmise that the Zodiacal Pattern first intimated in Genesis 1:14 holds an ancient key of confirmation that by intent, has been disguised (Whether intentional or not) from antiquity. The suppression of which, has been fueled by the Religious fervor of those who dare vouchsafe, though secretly of a divine origin - all the while condemning as inherently pagan, those of us who search for their authenticity!

Could the Religious Masters have developed an alternate, albeit, cleverly disguised transliteration as a ploy to prevent you from accessing this very truth? If so, perhaps exposing that plan would confirm a diabolical scheme to sell a counterfeit Messiah who would build a counterfeit system while securing that lie within the wrappings of a 3rd Temple. Could this centuries old archetype, an endeavor supposedly; to unite Judeo-Christian factions have fallen prey to the deliberate misinterpretations of a Babylonian System designed as the final act on a worldwide stage of delusion?

Is it possible, in the midst of the confusion of Daniel 7:25 where we see a future Anti-Messiah *who seeks to change times and laws and the Saints are given into his hand* - that we realize this plan is connected to a false calendar of Appointed Times? Accordingly, and in eye-opening contrast, dear Reader what you are seeing introduced here regarding The Cyclical or Round Tabernacle as a central Time-keeping device uniting the entire Body of Messiah on the same Holy Calendar would stand in stark contrast would it not?

Frankly, if not convinced, can you argue with the following? If construction began tomorrow would the 3rd Temple, a place of pious worship notwithstanding, allow among its adherents those who welcome Yahshua the Messiah – the One whom the Church calls Jesus much less, receive those Outcasts of the House of Israel who undeniably worship Him? Sobering isn't it?

Strangely enough, in support of my conjecture regarding two-contrasting calendars and a Tabernacle versus Temple architecture, perchance you'd give attention to the word translated above as 'Saints': It is transcribed from H#6922 (An Aramaic derivative of Hebrew) and written: קַדִּישׁ, qaddiysh. Despite being translated 'holy or separate' here, it is equally used of ANGELS, and in essence could indicate the Living Beings! Consequently in relation to the *changing of 'times'* by the Anti-Messiah – in this manner, it links the two as a Zodiacal Timekeeping mechanism.

This would undeniably produce a perverted Sacred Calendar, which would have to reconcile with its 3rd Temple counterpart! Frankly, at this writing the Jewish year is designated 5781. Further, its existence is one commonly known deliberately and candidly to be at least 240 plus Years off! As I state this, in the interest of a counter-balance regarding any accusations of anti-Semitic bias, I vigorously assert that the Roman calendar together with the Grecian and Arabic influence on the Zodiac is also pointedly ambiguous! Accordingly, as proponents of Scriptural integrity we must conclude that something is amiss!

If Abba declares that He is restoring a pure language (Zephaniah 3:8) then the keys to understanding and correcting those calculations, at least from a textural perspective exists! Additional extra-biblical, historical Clues hidden for centuries are also being revealed allowing us to decipher the correct Heavenly Prophetic Pattern! Stand firm my Brothers as the King of Creation reveals His Plans, which were etched in the Heavens before the foundations of this planet were laid!

Chapter 3

The Heavenly Prophetic Pattern and Genesis 3

This scene we've addressed in Genesis chapter 3 as depicted in the Pattern of the Heavenlies is found illustrated in the Constellational Decan called Cepheus, situated in the House of Pisces, itself located just beneath the North Star – Polaris – at the celestial pole. This Pole Star position has changed since the compilation of Genesis 3 and will change again because of the 2160-year Zodiacal rotational ecliptic.

Hence, 1,000 years from now, Cepheus will become the True North Star…Cepheus is a compilation of Stars configured as ONE SITTING ON A THRONE RULING OVER THE OTHER 12-HOUSES! His foot is depicted as resting on the head of the Pole star where Drago currently sits as prophesied in Gen. 3:15:

> *And I will put enmity between thee and the woman, and between thy seed and her seed; it shall bruise thy head, and thou shalt bruise his heel.*

Cepheus in Hebrew is rendered Tzemach – The Branch - and is paired with Cassiopeia his Queen in the sign of Aries. She is depicted as the Captive who is delivered to become the Bride! Yahshua came to do just that in Genesis 3! His, Cepheus' objective, is to set free His collective Bride – Adam and Chavah-Eve – who have been ensnared by the Dragon, that Old Serpent, the Devil!

**Note: See Revelation 12:9 and 20:2.

By the way, before going further, in the interest of clarity let me return briefly to spotlight a key portion of the phrase describing the tasks assigned to Adam in Gen. 2:15 where he is said *'to dress and keep'* – avad v'shamar - the garden: Those words in Hebrew are inherently, without doubt, PRIESTLY TERMS! If, dear Reader, there are (perhaps you will accede to it) numerous references defining our own role as ostensibly that of a Nation or kingdom of priests. Then, I will argue, if true, our primary function should seemingly be confined to that of attending Him in worship, He who is our God and at His discretion, not ours! Those same holy seasons are none other presumably, than the biblically prescribed, set-times found in Leviticus 23 and defined by the Creator as "My Feasts" a Holy Writ, in effect nullifying any man-made substitutes, would you not also agree?

As such, one would not deign to address it as our solemn DUTY – one to be held sacrosanct, though the lens of tradition seems focused on an illegitimate offender who has usurped the role that is JOSPEH'S BY INHERITANCE! Perchance, you'll as well agree this sacred employment requires firsthand knowledge of His schedule?

> *And ye shall be unto me a kingdom of priests, and an holy nation. These are the words, which thou shalt speak unto the children of Israel.* Exodus 19:6

**Note: See also 1Peter 2:5, 9 and Revelation 1:6, 5:10.

As we connect the dots of collaborative information, from Genesis forward, it looks as if Adam was placed in the center of Gan Eden, which could just as easily have been called 'the garden of The Circle of Time' – After The Pattern of the Heavens! Adam, then would function much like the Sun mentioned by the Psalmist in chapter 19:5, 6 – where his (The Sun's) prescribed role is as a *bridegroom coming out of his chamber. His going forth is from the ends of the heaven, and his circuit unto the ends of it: and there is nothing hid from the heat thereof.* – He would purposely have to move in and out of the Cycles of the House(s) of the Zodiacal Signs while observing the Appointed Times or Convocations set by them!

Therefore, Adam in his created role seems to function like the mechanized *'hands of a clock'* - but for what purpose? Remember, Adam is a shadow picture of the first ET – the Aleph-Tav – The First Extra Terrestrial!

On the face of this body of evidence, I propose that a physical body, like ours, bound to the dimensions of time and space, inasmuch as our religious traditions dictate what we currently see, was not what you'd expect and that our current out of the box thinking leaves us contemplating a physical world which originally **would not have limited Adam**!

Accordingly, it is my opinion that Adam was able to "time-travel" – i.e. he could enter a portal at a specific time (Perhaps during a Holy Convocation – H#4744, Miqra) and move, travel without limits. In fact, I declare emphatically: *He was the original Time Traveler*! Skeptical? Perhaps you are, but dear Reader, being thunderstruck by my observations doesn't negate the overwhelming evidence in support! What? Evidence? In my bible you ask? Yes, (Yawn…loud sighing) in that dusty, old family album on your nightstand lies a treasure trove of stunning revelation only waiting for you to extricate it!

By the same token, we have numerous Biblical records after the Fall, of those limitations being suspended and a "mortal" man doing just that! Enoch (Walked with God and was not, for God took him) Moshe (80 days without food and water left him in a different physiological state) Elijah (He is translated on more than one occasion, the final one in a whirlwind encounter with a fiery chariot, much like the wind surrounding Ezekiel's Wheel Within a Wheel) Yahshua (Upon the Mount of Transfiguration and once when He becomes invisible to a group attempting to stone Him) Paul (His out-of-body experience) and Phillip (Translated to an encounter with an Ethiopian Eunuch!)

If each of these men *"seemingly defied the laws of physics"* by transcending normal time/space boundaries in order to accomplish the vision given them, isn't it entirely plausible that the Future potential for catastrophic events may require individuals and perhaps even companies of people to be moved out of harm's way into the sanctuary – Tabernacle of YHVH's Appointed times in much the same manner?

Isn't it also rational of us to assume that if the *First Time Traveler* – Adam – is accosted in his efforts by the Serpent of Genesis 3 (Who really wasn't a land-crawling, reptilian entity, but instead a sooth-saying, word twisting liar, who just happened to drop by unexpectedly while Adam and Chavah – Eve are preparing for an intimate visit – *sarcasm mine*) how could we not in all conscience expect a future with no less of either Time-travel or opposition?

As it happens, The Creator uses archetype, patterns, and repetition in order to facilitate learning. Each is a contrivance providing a historical affidavit of witness for future generations to learn from. Isn't it therefore possible, reminiscent of the Genesis 3 record that a future Counterfeit "Serpent-Messiah-Temple" (A pseudonym of the Great Triad of Deception) would look to intervene at a forthcoming, predestined venue for the purpose of compromising or counterfeiting the Plan of YHVH? What events could ensure such an occasion?

Would the cracking of the Wheel Within the Wheel Code? Maybe decrypting the language of the Wilderness Tabernacle thus unveiling a Cyclical-Round Tabernacle of Meeting, pray tell?

Would the locating of Gan Eden, the Garden of Appointed Times be the instrument to start a domino effect?

Each of these are events of paramount importance and able alone to change the course of a United Believing Community, but what if each occurred simultaneously at a predetermined signal of release? The probability of a tsunami-like tidal wave of revelation is astronomical in its proportions, yet it is in front of you NOW! You have in your hands a historic, cyclical template that has been lost to understanding for generations now being restored to this GENERATION! HALELUYAH!

If the potential for the above exists, then, while we are excited and reveling in His Glory, at the same time a certain prognostic ambience settles upon those who are vigilant, the group who are destined Watchmen on the Wall! We must be careful of our hearing. For it is filtered through the vestige of the flesh. To our chagrin, the flesh loves tradition more than truth. When facing the challenge of fresh revelation and accepting that we need change, more often than not, the proverbial 'sow returns to its wallow'.

Tradition needs challenge, for our sake and for that of future generations. From my personal standpoint, I believe the pursuit of religious tradition produces an inbred colony that are willing to insulate themselves by whatever means from the Purest Stock whose DNA is Torah.

Should change come, it inevitably challenges our comforts. This should be a warning. If you're uncomfortable, remember: Truth can stand scrutiny, traditions often cannot. If our eschatological future depends on rightly dividing the word of truth, then we must vigorously prosecute the religious paradigm keeping us in the Dark Ages when we could be free. Ignorance is not freedom. Let me share Proverbs 4:7:

Wisdom is the principal thing; therefore get wisdom: and with all thy getting get understanding.

In the shadows of the challenge just issued regarding the pursuit of understanding, perhaps I have left you scratching your noggin as you wonder where that lick came from. I'll share the following verses with you that have indeed been hemmed in by that ugly word 'tradition'. You see, the pursuit of truth is accomplished the fastest when we allow someone to run after it for us. (*Sarcasm mine*). That being said, this is a life and death situation! As you read the next paragraph, stop and think of the doom and gloom scenarios you are patently familiar with. Then bear in mind after you read what is truthfully being shown, that you paid your tithes and offerings in order to find yourself a card-carrying member of a bamboozled congregation! Bwahahahaha! Seriously, this won't hurt long!

And except those days should be shortened, there should no flesh be saved: but for the elect's sake those days shall be shortened. Matthew 24:22 and Mark 13:20

Mark says, "Except the Lord shortened". This is not speaking of shortening, curtailing, abridging, or the pruning of the 24-hour day, but rather, the days - cumulative, i.e. the year. It is my considered opinion that the Circular Tabernacle Pattern, the alignment of the Stars, their incremental association with specific Holy Days all reveal the Plan of the Creator to once again provide for His People a venue [Time and Place] in which to have access to Him for intimacy, Worship, Protection, etc.

It is highly probable that the return to a 360-day calendar will be the device that allows for the Outcasts of Israel to be afforded protection at certain times much like what we read in the apocalyptic details of Revelation 12:14, another verse obscured by the Puritanical minds who tell us we shouldn't study the Zodiacal Signs! Can you hear the Freedom Train coming?

> *And to the woman were given two wings of a great eagle, that she might fly into the wilderness, into her place, where she is nourished for a time, and times, and half a time, from the face of the serpent.*

This is the same woman a few verses earlier appearing clothed with the Sun, the moon under her feet, and having a crown of 12 stars. This is none other than the constellation Virgo-Bethulah! Curiously, this sign occurs quite often during the month of Tishrei where on day 1 we celebrate Rosh Hashanah – the Festival of Trumpets! Followed by 10 days of AWE leading to Yom Kippur – the Day of Covering – Hiding – Protecting!

Incidentally, the Half-Torah portion read during this season includes Zechariah's thermonuclear war description found in Zechariah 5:9 where the words translated 'two women' could also be rendered TWO FIRES with wings like a stork! The Hebrew word for women H#802 אשה, ishshah, can etymologically be traced to the word for Fire offering! Note verse 8:

> *And he said, This is wickedness. And he cast it into the midst of the Ephah; and he cast the weight of lead upon the mouth thereof.*

Nuclear warheads were originally lined with lead. Both the US and UK initially used casings made of steel, which were lined with lead or a lead bismuth alloy to form the radiation case (probably 1-3 cm thick). The secondary pusher, which made up the inner wall of the radiation channel, was made of either natural uranium or lead (again, possibly as a lead-bismuth alloy). Operational bombs probably all used uranium tampers to maximize yield, but some test devices were equipped with lead tampers to hold down yield and fallout production. A massive radiation shield (uranium or lead) was located between the primary and secondary to prevent fuel preheating by the thermal radiation flux. A boron neutron shield was used in some designs to reduce neutron preheating.

You see, I only shared the above as an additional example of how the eyepiece of tradition is often inclined to something quite different than what is really hidden in the text. Though the ancient Scribes would have had no understanding of the future import of such a description, the fact is, prudence begs us to review our closely held beliefs through the ever-changing, chameleon-like lens of understanding! Does this mean that YHVH changes His Word! NO! It does however mean that we tend to view Scripture through the shortsighted lens shaped by a man's perspective of what that Word supposedly meant! Does this make sense?

Honestly though, in their defense, Church scholars do not have an adequate perspective of these events, simply because of having been purposely alienated from the confirmation that can be found in the Zodiacal Message! Point of fact: Their message, is older, factual, tested and consequently, were we seeking a Lawful-Court room opinion, evidential standing carries weight – first in Time – first in Right - it's presentment of fact, thus superseding any attestation submitted afterward! In support, let me show you the conclusion of the matter from a worldly jurisdiction. *#5

Now, as we return to our discussion of the arcane narrative of the woman found in Revelation 12: You will undoubtedly find - in how we break the text down - an affirmation of sorts, regarding what we're claiming.

As we continue, your orientation dear Reader will change, in

---

* #5. *These past decisions are called "case law", or* precedent. Stare decisis—*a Latin phrase meaning "let the decision stand"—is the principle by which judges are bound to such past decisions.*
https://en.wikipedia.org/wiki/Case_law - Public Domain

part, because the revelatory nature of the story of this Sun-Clothed Woman will now also seemingly *'change'*. A position from whence, you will view her as she was intended to be portrayed and that from her rightful station which incorporates an awareness brought from the Message in the Heavens. As a result, we are accommodating the Reader in a manner contextually and consistently found throughout Scripture! Please consider the following!

The Sun-Clothed Woman

She is initially brought into the Wilderness – B'midbar – a Hebrew phrase interpreted as; the House where the Word is Wombed – a place prepared for her in advance – the Gk. Word used, hetoimazo, means a Road leveled in advance for her passage! Interestingly, the word Zodiac translates also as 'The Way' or The Road! Context seems to indicate that She will be nurtured, supported, or strengthened 'while traversing' this Way-Road! Further, we are told 'they will feed her there': This word for 'feed' comes from the Greek word Gk.5157, Trope - meaning a turning or revolution of the heavenly bodies - perhaps for 1260 days, 42 months?

These numbers are not accidental! They are manifestly seen revealing a 360-day calendar! Can you hear me Reader? She *flees into the Wilderness*...the Greek word used here for 'flee' is G#5343, pheugo, and by analogy implies that she was in the throes of abhorrent danger and *vanished safely out of harm's way*! Vanished?

Doesn't this sound like the modus operandi of Ezekiel, Elijah, Moshe, Enoch, Yahshua, Paul and Phillip each of whom were 'miraculously transported' at a specific time? Might that be the very reason she enters the – Wormhole or time warp – the vehicle of destiny prepared for her at the exact moment in time that the earthly event synchronizes with the movement of the Stellar Timepiece called the Zodiac?

Now, if you're able to digest that, consider this. The moon is seen under her feet. The Greek word is rendered G#4582, selene, for its brilliancy. It is akin to G#138, haireo, to choose, prefer, to elect by a vote to an office. Strange choice of words isn't it? This doesn't give us much information. She is 'standing' on the moon, a full moon, which is significant. This 'standing' (From a Court of Law's perspective) indicating a foundation or position demonstrating the ability by sufficient connection to that Law that one may experience either relief or harm should that law be abrogated! What part then does this moon play? For clarity's sake it is my belief that the New Testament – especially Revelation, would have been originally written in Hebrew.

So, let's examine the Hebrew word for a Full Moon, H#3677, כסא, keh'seh. This is important, because a Full Moon – keh'seh – was a time keeping mechanism itself, indicating the festival appointment, as in Passover and/or Sukkot, the Feast of Tabernacles! Fasten your seatbelt! This same word with different vowel pointing – כסא, kicce' H#3678, is the Hebrew word for seat of honor or throne. Indicating royal dignity, authority and power! She is seen visibly portrayed in the heavens and this same archetype – Woman = Bride – the Bride of Messiah is demonstrating her right to intervention from and standing upon – the Throne of the King! This same 'Heavenly Vision' given to John the Revelator is contextually consistent with the dream of Joseph where the Sun, Moon and Stars, bow at his feet! To bow is to acknowledge the sovereign Standing of the one approached!

It is my contention that the Outcast House of Joseph, much like Gomer, (H#1586, גמר, defined as meaning Complete, to finish, to bring to an end) the harlot bride of Hosea, (H#1954, הושע, Salvation, the short form of Yahoshua or Yahshua, the Messiah) was a hidden clue regarding this Sun-Clothed woman whose covering will be transformed into the Brilliant Garments of the

Bride of Messiah and is being introduced here in Revelation chapter 12! She is in stark contrast to the Harlot Bride of chapter 17:3-7 identified as 'Mystery Babylon' also depicted in the Wilderness clothed in Scarlet robes of feigned royalty! Incidentally, Gomer has the same meaning as Kallah another Hebrew word for – Bride, 'it is finished'. Again, to bow is to acknowledge the sovereign Standing of the one approached!

As we've stipulated early on, by initiating this original pattern, the Sun-Clothed Woman, seen from the mirror of Genesis 3 is clothed, arrayed – has a status change, receives a new covering or authority. She no longer is slave to the Serpent or the Dragon of Revelation chapter 12, the very moment when the lamb is slaughtered to cover both she and her Ish – Husband Adam! He, who in a manner like the Sun (Psalm 19) would move into and out of, a new "Zodiacal House" at *each 30-day PRIESTLY cycle!* Hmmmm?

The Torah illustrates this picture of The Tabernacle Man lying upon the earth while being circumscribed by the Heavenlies in the person of Adam, Isaac, Jacob, Messiah and the Wilderness Tabernacle. Curiously, many of the learned men of antiquity also considered this "Tabernacle – As a Man Within a Circle": One of the more familiar, though we may not connect him to the Wheel Within the Wheel, is Leonardo DaVinci.

His intriguing artwork reveals a physical link to what is otherwise a spiritual supposition on my part. One, we believe the Living Beings of Ezekiel to be indicative of the Stellar Luminaries as characterized in the Ancient portrayal of the Zodiacal Signs. Two, we contend, that Ezekiel is being shown an earthly answer to what was entirely a heavenly pattern. In other words, an earthly template existed that must be withdrawn from religious, traditional ambiguity, and attention called to it as a second witness corroborating the Redemption plan of the Creator. The message has lain in dust-covered obscurity until now! We must revisit our conception of both the heavenly and earthly patterns else we become prey to the delusional flood vomited out of the mouth of the Dragon of Revelation 12! Prepare the Way of the King!

DaVinci's Vitruvian Man *#6

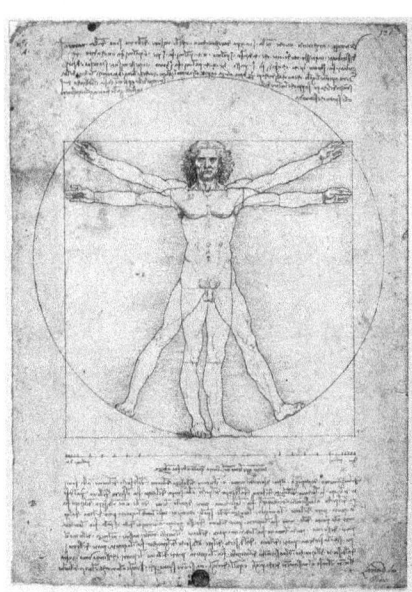

Leonardo is clearly illustrating Vitruvius De Architectura 3.1.3, which reads:

> *The navel is naturally placed in the centre of the human body, and, if in a man lying with his face upward, and his hands and feet extended, from his navel as the centre, a circle be described, it will touch his fingers and toes. It is not alone by a circle, that the human body is thus circumscribed, as may be seen by placing it within a*

---

* #6. Note: This image of DaVinci's Vitruvian Man is in the public domain and is used herein without malice:
https://commons.wikimedia.org/wiki/File:Vitruvian.jpg

square. For measuring from the feet to the crown of the head, and then across the arms fully extended, we find the latter measure equal to the former; so that lines at right angles to each other, enclosing the figure, will form a square.

Chapter 4

The Tabernacle –
The Man Inside the Wheel Within the Wheel

Another of the more famous Scriptural illustrations of the *Man Within The Circle* – I.E. the Man inside the Wheel Within the Wheel is none other than that of Jacob who flees his brother Esau, to later arrive at the 'Place' – H#4725, מקום, pronounced as; Maqowm. This was not an ordinary place, but, rather, an emphatic "THE PLACE"!

Let's stop here a moment. Once again our traditional conceptual analysis of this story, leaves much to be desired in the way of Truth. We are simply not told the possibility of an antediluvian connection. Nor, are we made to understand much about what is to transpire here! Again, The Creator is habitual, thorough in His utilization of parabolic (Symbols common to the hearer) methods, repetition, and rote learning as a mechanism to convey the message. Those methods do not deviate here.

On the basis thereof, the evidence about to be presented you, strongly suggests this was the location of Gan Eden! One of its aliases that of: The Garden of Appointed Times. Taken into consideration, that Eden existed as the Womb of Creation, the repository of the DNA of all living, then it isn't a stretch to anticipate a set-time when the Creator arrives via the Portal between the Heavens and Earth, between the spiritual and physical realm. Which became, to borrow the words immortalized by Led Zeppelin - a literal 'Stairway to Heaven'! This Being is seen in Genesis 3 as The Voice, or The Word. It is the Word that contains the DNA! It is the Word alone that has the power to repair a broken DNA helix! Now, consider this:

As a result, this Maqowm or place forever became the vanguard of a universal evangelistic effort to restore creation from its fallen condition to that of a Restored-Renewed and Redeemed status! Adam and simultaneously Eve – Chavah experience this firsthand. They are initially formed out of the DNA of Elohiym only to experience the fall. The resulting metastasis, that deadly contagion known as sin immediately begins its virulent crusade to circumvent the ability of those Sons of The Living Elohiym - bearers of the Name or lineage of the Creator (Passed to Adam) from exercising rightful authority over his inheritance!

Thus, a Promise of One Who Would Come – becomes the Living Hope of that Creation! Fast-forward and we now have Jacob found here in Genesis 28 experiencing the dream of the ladder! Can you say PORTAL, WORMHOLE, and TIME-TRAVELER? Incredibly, are we witnessing Creation's first Déjà vu? Jacob sees The Voice, The Word ascending and descending upon what is literally a DNA HELIX! Not entirely persuaded?

Let me present you a couple of pictures of a helix.

**Note their structure one of which, looks eerily like a center wheel between two others! Wait? Or, perhaps, the one on the right a top-down look into a Wheel Within a Wheel? *#7A, #7B

---

* #7A. DNA Double Helix by Jerome Walker, Dennis Myts is in the Public Domain and is used herein without malice.
https://commons.wikimedia.org/wiki/File:DNA_double_helix_45.PNG
#7B. DNA Helix Amino Acids Biology by LJNovaScotia is in the Public Domain and is used herein without malice.
https://pixabay.com/illustrations/dna-helix-amino-acids-biology-4574319

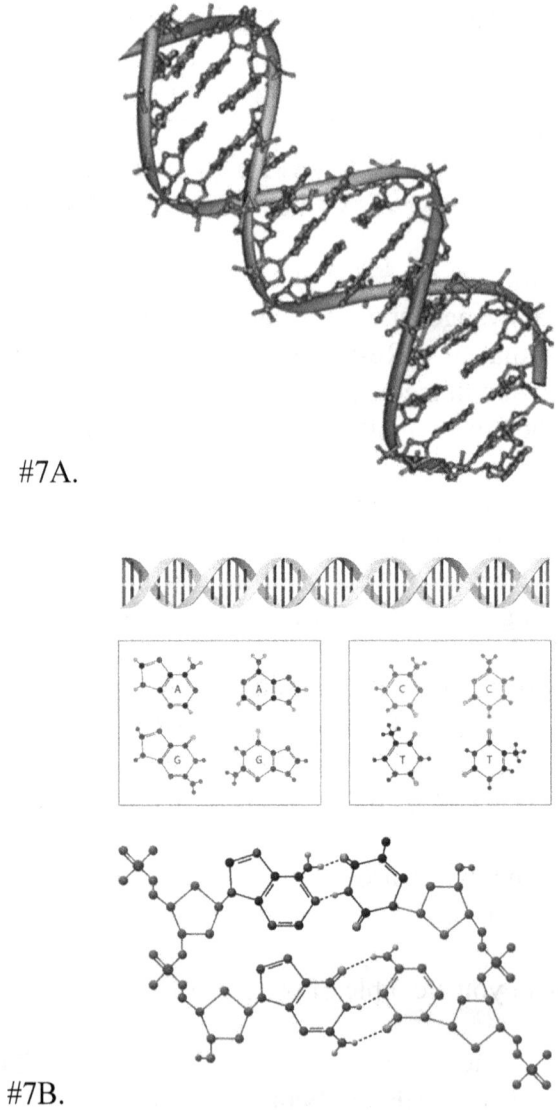

#7A.

#7B.

The Hebrew of the Genesis 28:11 account tells us Jacob took מאבני, m'ebeni – eben being the word for stones; while the pictograph of the Mem indicates a womb – the loins - of that place, Maqowm and put them for his pillows, H#4763, מראשות, merashote: Again, Mem – is a womb, to encircle. It becomes entirely likely that he encircled his head with the stones: What stones? Now, look at the root of merashote. It is cognate with, related to, reshiyt – the Beginning or Head, from the same root as B'reshiyt – In The Beginnings! Was Jacob being shown the blueprint of Eden, the Message in the Heavens that would be confirmed in the earth through his seed? While Jacob languishes upon the earth, perhaps in a spread-eagle form doesn't it give rise to a subliminal nod toward DaVinci's illustration, causing it to look eerily familiar?

This is quite intriguing, considering that Jacob not only mimicked the pattern by lying down at the Maqowm or Place, where he slept, shakab, to rest, to lie with someone sexually, but later set up a memorial pillar, H#4676, מצבה, Matstsebah, Mem = womb, origin, while the root Tzav, indicates HOST – as in host of heavens, further, the two-letter stem Tzade-Bet indicates a vehicle of transportation! COULD JACOB HAVE SEEN THE WHEEL WITHIN THE WHEEL EVEN BEFORE EZEKIEL???

To add further confirmation, the events that follow cannot simply be random acts. For example, upon awakening Jacob travels to the land of the people of the east. [The Garden was EASTWARD in Eden] Here he encounters 3 flocks of sheep lying by a well with a stone upon it. Jacob opens the well and waters the sheep of Rachael.

I find this far from coincidental! In fact, purely astonishing! Why? Because once again, the average Reader having been alienated from the ancient Witness of the Stars, those Signs in the heavens consistent with the 12 Houses of the Zodiac, will not understand what is transpiring at this scene here at the well. Nor, for that matter, will most realize that here, the physical actions of Jacob follow that same heavenly template portrayed in the heavens shown to his father Abraham in Genesis 15 regarding Jacob/Israel and his 12 sons!

In this particular instance, the Redemptive message portrays him in a role consistent with that of the future Messiah! By drawing water for Rachel Jacob represents Aquarius, or in Hebrew, Deli, known more commonly as the Water Bearer. The Flocks represent Cancer or Klaria – the Sheepfold and Rachel – Virgo or Bethulah the Virgin!

What we're seeing is Prophetic! Aquarius the Water Bearer symbolizes the Living Water. The Living Seed planted into the Virgin and thus, producing the Flock! This was a prophetic declaration attested to by the Zodiacal Signs! It was also further confirmation of the encounter at THE MAQOWM – THE PLACE WHERE JACOB'S DREAM OCCURS AND WHERE HE FIRST SAW THE DNA OF THE LIVING WATER – WORD testifying of what would become his promised Seed! How ironic - as the Zodiacal Ecliptic turns after its 2160-year cycle - that we're now about to enter the "Age of Aquarius", where the Bride will deliver the Sheepfold to the King!

Once more, since I understand the difficulty of change and supposing that the lens of tradition remains yet a bit foggy, due diligence requires connecting the proverbial 'dots' linking Jacob to the Wheel Within the Wheel. Whereas names are the most condensed prophetic summary known to man, we should investigate the origin of Jacob's name to see if perhaps the conventional translation could have been a Weapon of Mass Confusion in order to misdirect the future generations!

Let's do a bit of etymological detective work here. We know the routinely accepted definition of Jacob, H#3290, יעקב, right? I'm sure you're familiar with Heel catcher, supplanter, deceiver, etc.? These definitions are easily attributable to Jacob's elder brother Esau. Indeed, it is from his carnal, chimerical nature – coupled with a bitter and vitriolic hatred of his brother – that Esau spoke these! Further, that we've accepted ignorantly these spoken, undefended words I believe Esau to have vomited is truly why, a wholly negative legacy is foisted upon Jacob/Israel! Launching in essence, an attack of generational proportions! Incredibly this, in the aftermath of his having sold to Jacob his First Born inheritance and secondly, his role as the True Priest of the family! *This friend; is the lens of tradition!* We simply cannot accept such at its face value! Duty of care becomes the sieve through which we meticulously examine these seeds of prophetic DNA; else our own legacy as Sons of Israel remains tainted!

Consequently, our addiction to the hidden truths found in the Hebrew letters prompts a more thorough examination of the name and simultaneously, the reputation previously formed by *misinterpretation*! The lynchpin of our investigation must focus at the Qof-Bet-Vet qavav, root stem of Y'aqob, which hints at being elevated, a mound, an arched vault, and an erected tent! Was he, like Adam, and, like Messiah intended to be the Man depicted in the Elevated Tent in the Arched Vault of Heaven – The Ohel Mo'ed – The Man in the Tent of Appointed Times – The Man in The Written DNA of the STARS?

This Tent of Meeting is circular not rectangular or square! Why is this important? If true, this divulges information regarding the genuine identity of Jacob (Also known as Israel, and in particular the reason(s) for their later dispersal) previously known only to few and therefore, intended to be kept secret until a specific season in the future! Did you see this coming dear Reader?

Against this background, the Qof-Bet-Vet root is revealing! The Rabbis say that the Hebrew letter Qof depicts a Monkey; as in Monkey see - monkey do. ***The Qof means to imitate, to copy, while the Double letter 'bet' indicates the 2 houses! Jacob's true hidden purpose was/is to expose the Counterfeit that is dividing the 2 Houses of Israel***! It is this religious counterfeit which has today taken on the identity of Esau; much as Jacob did in the ruse by which he disguised himself in the garments of Esau in order to take back what had been promised: *The Elder shall serve the Younger*!

Could this Circular Pattern in the heavenlies, the Circular Tent in the Wilderness, the 360-day calendar, the cyclical restoration of the Festival Appointments, the Restoration of the CYCLICAL DNA LANGUAGE OF YHVH – HEBREW, ALL be keys hidden until this season in order to expose the counterfeits within this latter day House of Israel? Allow me to take a short aside here to reveal some life-altering information!

Did You Know? – I'll Bet You Didn't

Our literary side trip here is in a rather unusual, unfamiliar place. I dare say, you will wonder the merit of our tangent for only a short few minutes! Our destination? The Government Styles Manual!

This is a rather little known compendium outside a select group, which sets standards and procedures for Script – legal and/or otherwise, and which states that any word, phrase or symbol set apart from the page by Brackets [ ] parenthesis ( ) *italics* or a square is said to NOT EXIST on that page legally! I have to urge you to prepare for what follows and please don't waste this Book! At least use it as a coffee coaster until you are sufficiently resuscitated!

If the above notations have a hidden agenda within public and private text, known only to a privy few, then *what does this say for the Square/rectangular pattern of the 3rd Temple a pattern not consistent with the original design of the Wilderness Tent of Meeting? If what is contained within the above-described symbols is said to legally 'not exist' what then, becomes of the Deity worshipped or inscribed within that squared tabernacle symbol? Does He also not exist?*

Call me Conspiratorial if you want, but, Truth will stand scrutiny – the counterfeit requires none! In order to solidify our position, and at the same time, not presume the Reader easily swayed; we will heap a mountain of evidence upon you, from within the confines of this book and allow you the decision-making! For

David Mathews

starters….

Let's Return to the Message of the Pattern in the Circle of Stars.

There are no scholarly arguments against the creation of the Stellar Luminaries and their first mention found in Genesis 1:14-18. The disagreement and resulting controversial positions wherein most scholars are traditionally root-bound stems from their inability to see the Luminaries as anything other than simply the Sun by day and the stars by night! You prayerfully, will enjoy a more cogent look than is customarily afforded them. At the conclusion of this journey, it is my hope that your perspective will have its edges knocked off and you'll fit nicely into the round hole of what is now "traditional non-conformity!" ☺

What exactly are these luminaries and for what purpose were they created? Merely to divide day from night and for signs, seasons, days and years, to rule the day and night? Before you spout off your knee jerk, nicely packaged, religiously pious, Sunday school rehearsed "I don't Know" (Gotcha) let's devote some skin to the game and do a tad bit of meticulous Word Surgery before coming to a conclusion! I want to call attention to several key words: But, first let me stipulate that the Moon is NOT A LUMINARY – It has no light of its own!

**Note verse 16 of Genesis 1:

> *And God made two great lights; the greater light to rule the day, and the lesser light to rule the night: he made the stars also.*

The Hebrew word for light is ma'owr, H#3974, מָאוֹר, and can be singular or plural. Also, (Remember our Government Styles Manual?) the English italicized words *'he made'* are not in the text. The Hebrew transliterated into English literally reads: va'ET-haMa'owr haqatan, lemmeshalote halailah vET hakowkaviym!

As we continue, the Hebrew word for 'lesser' is H#6996, קָטָן, qatan, said to originate from the Qof-Vav root, which hints at 'lesser in size'. Remember the Qof-Vav is also the root of Jacob, Yaakov! It means to duplicate, to copy! The Moon had no light of its own, instead, it is the Stellar luminaries who would supply the duplicated, copied image in the Tent or Vault of the Heavens! In Passing, that same Qof-Vav root indicates a thread for measuring, as in a circle, and a zone!

From a practical standpoint, allowing an architectural purview of the above, if you were to place a center punch in the median of any project with a thread tied to it and a marker attached at its end you would have the means with which to transcribe a circle! In a similar manner, the luminaries transcribe the Zodiacal Circle and by the same token, the Qof-Vav root of 'lesser' forms a nexus linking us to the hidden role of Jacob, as the Man in the Center of the Wheel Within the Wheel - Time's Tabernacle or Dwelling Place!

Within this context, incorporating the explanation as we've extrapolated it for you, the above textural phrase of Genesis 1 verse 16 can in reality, be translated as: *And He made the lesser light(s) the stars, to rule the night*! The sun rules the day, the stars the night! Note the Hebrew word for rule, H#4475, מֶמְשָׁלָה, mamshalah, which is out of context based upon our observations above. This is made obvious as it originates from the root of mashal, to make like, to assimilate, a similitude, and also, a parable!

This is confirmed in Psalms 19 above where these stars are depicted as conveying a parabolic message in the similitude of the Sun/Son whose heavenly circuit reveals His Covenant Purpose whilst prophetically revealing the time frame or circular calendar at the set time these Covenant events were predetermined to occur!

For this reason, a massaged calendar, and/or a counterfeit Tabernacle design or any such change that compromises this Circular design may affect the Message; without forgetting the negative impact upon those who are able to attend the appointments! Perhaps this was deemed necessary by the Creator in order to expose both the Genuine and Counterfeit in attendance at those specific dates? Or mayhap, potentially allowed that the event or message remain disguised until the appointed time? This makes the arguments over the Calendar issue frivolous without knowing if the specific one we adhere to is correct! Is it??? Has there ever been a calendar change and if so, perhaps a future one? How would such affect the Believing Community? What exactly is the truth?

At least 4-yearly cycle calendar changes in History with another coming!

Most people get uncomfortable when discussing this possibility, yet both Biblical and ancient historical records detail such changes. Note Daniel's comments:

> *He changes the times and appointed moments. He reveals the deep and mysterious things…* Daniel 1:21-22

> *Declaring the end from the beginning and from ancient times the things that are not yet done, saying, My counsel shall stand, and I will do all my pleasure!* Isaiah 46:10

It is my opinion (Though not a casual one) that a Calendar change took place in the interim period between Genesis chapter 1:1, 2 and 1:14. It is here that Creation in a condition of Perfection from its inaugural beginning, is portrayed in verse 2 in a much lesser state, represented as "Without form and void" (KJV) תֹהוּ וָבֹהוּ transcribed as Tohu v'bohu in Hebrew.

These two verses have provided a platform whereupon generations of scholars camped in an effort best described as ambiguous at best! Yet, sensible analysis of the Hebrew yields quite another matter! For instance: This phrase has a numeric value of 430 - a very familiar number! In this capacity it is related to Nephesh – נֶפֶשׁ, those that breathe, live. Curiously, as we look at Nephesh, when the letter Nun is added as a prefix it indicates, incomplete action: As in 'we', we are, we will, while the Pey-Shin root hints at wickedness and direct rebellion against YHVH! Rebellion against YHVH is exactly what brought about the condition of Genesis 1:2!

Further, 430 is associated with the years between the offering of Isaac who foreshadowed Him and the Pesach Lamb seen 430 years later delivering Israel from the angel of death in Egypt! In fact, this was the very date given for the peculiar change introduced by Moshe to what had been Israel's calendar...*this shall be the beginning of months...* described in the text of Exodus 12:2!

I should also call to the Reader's attention that this 430-year time frame was a well-known event revealed in Exodus 12:41. How was this possible? Genesis 15:5 makes it very clear that Abraham was shown the message in the Stars and perhaps even the number of years leading up to that change! Otherwise, how could Abraham have known that he was in the later 5th -part of the 2160-year cycle known as the Precession of the Equinox already descending from the Decan or House of Taurus the Bull to that of Aries the Lamb? The template seen in the Zodiac is juxtaposed to the physical model on earth and revealed in the persons of Pharaoh (Seen as being translated as "House of the Bull – I.E. Apis and Hathor") and Moshe who would be seen in Aries as the prototypical Shepherd who is coming?

Second Calendar Change?

Further, 430 is the sum total of the combined years of exile assigned as judgment for both Judah (40) and Israel (390) in Ezekiel 4:1-6. As a result both are exiled from the Sabbath – the lynchpin of the Calendar of YHVH! Now, remember Yahshua, who is Himself described as the Lord of The Sabbath, is shown later openly declaring that *Sabbath was made for man* (Mark 2:27) and thus, following this pattern the 7th day Shabbat is observed being instituted immediately after creating or being made for, Adam - an event that seems to indicate that another change is being revealed where a second calendar is implemented to account for the structure of a 7-day Sabbath!

I understand! As incredulous sounding as this may be, the evidence is overwhelming – except for those who are content to *only see the trees and are thus blinded to the whole woods*! Please allow me an opportunity to expound before tossing this book again! By the way, how many times does this make? Yet, you still come back! That's because you have a destiny awaiting you! Now, let's penetrate the veil of tradition much deeper than most are comfortable with!

The creation of the Sabbath or Shabbat is seen occurring after *Genesis 1:14*, which initially reveals the Sun, Moon and Stars created to regulate the מועדים - Moedim, which only fits a 360-day, 12 months of 30 days calendar year! Don't take my word for this, just put a bookmark here and I'll come back and explain further.

Suffice it to say for the moment: These Moedim are cyclical appointments. In passing, let me also share that the root stem of moed comes from Yod-Ayin-Dalet, which can indicate to espouse a Wife; it is also the root of Eden, which we have already established as the garden of cyclical, appointed times! However, a significant alteration in how time is calculated (Solar, Lunar,

Stellar phases) seems to have been implemented and set into place after Adam's Body is created in Genesis 1: verses twenty-six and twenty-seven.

If I may interject here, the original timeline suggests, *time*, like the SABBATH was made for man and not vice-versa!

Consider examining the Hebrew of Genesis 2:1:

ויכלו השמים והארץ וכל-צבאם:

Transliterated as: V'yikalu hashamyim veh'arets vekal-tsavam – *Thus the heavens and the earth were finished, and all the host of them.* The key word to examine is the root Kaf-Lamed, kal; which can mean; all, to finish, complete, but also to hinder, to *restrain*, a cessation, and to hold back something that is to be prepared or made ready for someone.

How pertinent is this? The Shabbat's introduction follows immediately in verse two just after, where both the Sabbath and the Stellar 'Hosts' are introduced as that RESTRAINING FORCE! The Sabbath would help to regulate the calendar from this time forward in what seems like a 364-day year, 28-day lunar cycle.

Thus, this calendar was made ready for the Sabbath! In addition Enoch confirms to us that the calendar in use during his time was a 364-day Solar year, which would have fit perfectly with a 28-day lunar cycle and a 7-day week! Let's look here a minute in our next chapter!

Chapter 5

Enoch:
The Genuine and the Counterfeit!

The first time we see the name Enoch is in Genesis 4:17 hidden within the counterfeit lineage of Cain! Whereby we find the name of his first-born son revealed as H#2585, אֶת־חֲנוֹךְ, Et-Chanowk. The numeric value of Chanowk is 84, the same as the Hebrew word Yadah – to reveal, to make known, to make oneself known or to reveal oneself as! With the attached hyphenated Alef Tav, a curious spin is put on the phrase!

The Alef and Tav are the first and last letters of the Hebrew Script and as such were the chosen 'I AM' or Ego Eimi, Koine Greek *#8 appellation of Messiah Himself in the text of Revelation chapters 1, 21 and 22 where the Greek equivalent - Alpha and Omega – are shown. Thus, it isn't a fortuitous chance

---

* #8. *The Koine Greek term Ego eimi (Greek Ἐγώ εἰμί, pronounced [eγó imí]), literally **I am** or **It is I**, is an emphatic form of the copulative verb εἰμι that is recorded in the Gospels to have been spoken by Jesus on several occasions to refer to himself not with the role of a verb but playing the role of a name, in the Gospel of John occurring seven times with specific titles. These usages have been the subject of significant Christological analysis. The term I Am relating to God appears over 300 times in the Bible, first in the book of Genesis (15:1) and last in Revelation (22:16). This has led to the Biblical God sometimes being referred to as "the great 'I am'".*
https://en.wikipedia.org/wiki/Ego_eimi - Public Domain

or scribal error, but is intentionally inserted to call attention to this particular 'Enoch' the scion of Cain! He is the counterfeit Alef-Tav! His name means to train, initiate, discipline and to make a formal beginning, to install. From this, we know he was to introduce the Anti-Messiah! Interestingly the gematria of ET-Chanowk = 485, and is the same as: מקדשי אל – Miqdowshi El - EL's House or Tabernacle! Could the Mark of Cain and perhaps the Mark of the Beast be connected to a counterfeit Tabernacle, Festival Cycle? You decide!

It is worth noting that Enoch's father Cain, built a city, H#5892, עיר, iyr, [an encampment guarded by a watch: A keeping of time, one who watches or calls out the time] in NOD, the place of wandering, on the east-side of Eden, the Garden of appointed times! The Nun-Dalet root hints at rebellion, to incite, harlotry, and uncleanness! Nod, would have been the center of the Pagan harlot religious system and its worship as well as, a counterfeit to that established by the Creator! The City and its system produced a fraudulent Priestly Caste who established, inter alia, a forgery of the True Word – Torah, all while introducing bogus man-made 'holy-days' (holidays).

In passing, may I point out the word for Holy – Kadosh – is only one vowel different from Kadash, a temple prostitute! *Wait! Who're selling their bodies for Temple service, which service includes keeping the holy Appointments established by its Priestly Caste?* It is also interesting that this first Cain was (In establishing the City of Nod, his Priestly Caste and it's harlot system) in all candor, attempting to effect a counterfeit keeping of time on the EAST SIDE of the Circle or TABERNACLE OF EDEN!

As we continue, both extra biblical and Scriptural records attest to the bona fides of the second or righteous Enoch who is recorded to have helped safeguard the Pure Seed line through his role as chronicler of the Zodiacal calendar. This anti-deluvian most famous for 'walking with God' is introduced as the 7th from

Adam in Genesis 5:18. His father is named H#3382, ירד, Jared, meaning to go down, to decline in prominence.

Will the 364-day Solar year of Enoch's era decline or diminish in size? Thus, the two names Jared – Enoch indicate that something is about to be revealed that will cause another to decline in prominence! Is it the Enochian Calendar? Enoch dies at 365, (4 years before the birth of Noah) having lived 300 years after the birth of Methuselah, who lives 9-6-9 years and is 3-6-9 years old when Noah is born, while the flood begins in Noah's 6-0-0 year! Hinting at a 360-degree, cyclical calendar? Did you catch the sacred numbers? 3-6-9.

The Gematria or numeric values lend credence here as well! The KJV English phrase: *"And Enoch Walked with God"* as it is transliterated into Hebrew reads: ויתהלך חנוך את-האלהים - V'yitehalek Chanowk ET-H'Elohiym. Its value 1047, is the same as the phrase: שש-מאות shesh me'owt – 600 years, as in the 600th – year of Noah's life and synchronous with the date the Biblical account of the flood supposedly started! Though assumed by some as coincidental, the Prophetic nature of the Names and the timing of these events prove they could only have been calculated had the means of an accurate measure of time been provided!

Consider how manageable a calendar would be if YHVH did indeed institute one with a 360-day cycle! For example, 360 is divisible by many numbers including those especially helpful (in bold, even today) for calendars and timekeeping: **2**, **3**, **4**, 5, **6**, **8**, **9**, 10, **12**, **15**, **18**, **20**, **24**, **30**, 36, 40, **45**, **60**, 72, **90**, **120**, and **180**. It is also no secret that many of the eschatological dates, such as 1260, 1290, 1330, 3 ½ years, 42 months are inexorably linked to this specific chronometer! Moreover, a calendar year of 360 days is reasonably divisible when determining the 2 equinoxes, 2 solstices, four seasons, 12 months, not to mention ascribing 24 hours to the day, 24 time zones of 15 nominal degrees each, 60 minutes in an hour, and 60 seconds in a minute.

The evidence is ancient in origin and it is highly likely that Enoch is responsible for passing along the info regarding the approaching calendar change in the aftermath of the Great Deluge and for preparing his grandson Methuselah who subsequently passed it to Noah!

The more the light is shined on these hidden conformational nuggets, the more I find myself engrossed in looking for others! There seems no end to the prophetical revelation corroborating these Truths! Included in this group are the interesting accounts of Noah's grandfather and the interpretation of his Hebrew name: Methuselah, H#4968, מתושלח a compound word formed from the root stem of Mem-Tav often translated Met – death. Some scholars see this root in such words, which do indicate death, mortal man, etc. Yet, it more accurately evinces a specific, incremental partitioning of time, such as: 'when' or how long, an extension or space of time.

What is more, there is an intensity added when we consider the suffixed 3-letter root Shin-Lamed-Chet, pronounced shalach and translated as: to send, shoot forth, and give over, to inform by messenger. Not only that, but the tri-letter root can also suggest 'One who deals with skins, flesh, namely, tent coverings'! Armed with such information we should ask ourselves if the translation of his name is simply a foreboding premonition or perhaps more accurately a predilection based on Enoch's experience with the Zodiacal Witnesses, their cyclical counterparts and thus, founded upon his calculations of the calendar.

Indeed, could 'Methuselah' be a prophetic declaration of a calendar change scheduled to occur at his demise? Interestingly, the root shalach is seen in the Hebrew word for Table found in the Tabernacle Holy place: Table – Shulchan, שֻׁלְחָן, the Table of shewbread. Now this is thought provoking! Let me explain…

David Mathews

This Shulchan - table would most likely have been of a round design itself as it held the lechem hapaniym, a.k.a. The Bread of Faces, those 12-loaves of 'shewbread'. As a supplementary fact these loaves were baked in a Circular Design. This could quite possibly leave us *with an individual loaf sitting at each of the 12-1-2-3, positions around the table, in order to form a circular timepiece or clock face!* The 12-loaves would thus follow the heavenly alignment as well as, the pattern of the earthly Tabernacle harmonizing with the 12 tribes in their positions around the throne or celestial body! Much like their counterparts depicted in the Wilderness Tabernacle design!

There is one more Tabernacle article that I believe to have represented the ROUND – CELESTIAL Tabernacle in the heavens and that is the MENORAH with its 7 branches. This well-known article has been accepted from ancient times as representing the 7 visible planets together with, the 7 primary colors of the Rainbow as seen in Noah's day! Moreover, if we number the knops, flowers and bowls on each branch the resulting 12-3-6-9-clock face is visible!

* #9.

---

* #9. Human Tafel - Deutsch: Tafel 21 von Georg Humanns „Die Kunstwerke der Münsterkirche zu Essen": Siebenarmiger Leuchter (973-1011) is in the Public Domain and is used herein without malice. Source:
https://commons.wikimedia.org/wiki/File%3AHumann_Tafel_21.JPG

Enoch Instructs Noah Regarding A 360-Day Year

As we continue, from what we've been shown above, Noah seems to have been well informed regarding celestial events, calendars, and their influence on timekeeping. That being said, the flood, H#3999, מבול, mabbuwl, seems the catalyst for the return to a 360-day calendar here in Genesis 6:17. I found it fascinating that the gematria for Mabbuwl (78) is the same as the Hebrew word, H#1552, גלילה, gliylah, which was also the name of the Circular boundary or district around Ezekiel's temple! Gliylah contains the root stem galiyl, translated as to roll away, a circle; it is also the physical root of the place where Yahshua began His ministry - Galilee!

Mabbuwl also contains the root Mem-Vav-Lamed, muwl, to cut off, circumcise! This is consistent with the 364-day year being circumcised by 4 days! 4x24=96. 9 and 6 represent the living numbers [3-6-9] and the west-east orientation of the cardinal compass!

This idea of a change to a 360-day calendar seems substantiated by Noah's use of the 'Numbered' months in Genesis 7:11 (2nd) Genesis 8:4 (7th) and Genesis 8:5 (10th). And in Genesis 7:24 where the waters prevailed upon the earth a hundred and fifty days (5 months from the 2nd to the 7th month) of 30 days! Now, here is where it gets interesting! Remember it is in Exodus 12 where YHVH changes the order of the months, the first month becoming Nissan, the 7th being Tishrei. However, here it's the opposite!

Genesis 8:4 speaks of the Ark resting on Mt. Ararat on the 7th month, which would have been Nissan (first month in Exodus 12) and the 17th day, corresponding to the Festival of First fruits occurring 3 days, the 17th, after the Crucifixion of Messiah on the 14th of Nissan! Incidentally, Ararat is translated as: The Curse reversed!

Genesis 8:5 reveals the Ark rested until the 10th month (3rd month in Exodus 12) on the first day when the tops of the mountains were visible. The Hebrew word used here for Top, is H#7218, ראש, roshe, rendered top or head which, in passing, is also translated "Dog-Star" as found in Job 38:13, 15. The Dog Star is another name for Sirius. This was no anomaly! Nor was it a textural aberration, though the KJV translators treat the Hebrew with suspicion.

No doubt Noah who became the first known maritime sailor would have been familiar with Sirius as a navigational point situated against the mountaintop, its fixed position a common reference point for Astronomical observation! Sirius being the brightest star in the heavens notwithstanding, the additional emphasis of being the only star with a fixed 365.25-day solar calendar only adds conviction to the probability of its having served as a reference point in the face of the climatic changes brought about by the flood and subsequent return to a renewed 360-day solar year!

If not convinced yet, Noah is given a specific sign of this 'renewed' Covenant Calendar of 360 days in Genesis 8:22 where he is told:

> *While the earth remaineth, seedtime and harvest, and cold and heat, and summer and winter, and day and night shall not cease.*

Repeatedly, the KJV translation diminishes the integrity of what is, in fact, a powerful revelation waiting for the renaissance of the Hebrew Tongue – the Language of Creation! The reemergence of Hebrew in the last decade as a code-breaking study tool cannot be overemphasized! Its use accords us with a unique perspective as we consider the above verse!

The author is giving us fixed positional compass points and a time-keeping mechanism as he speaks of the 2 cardinal equinoxes of spring and fall and the 2 solstices (Summer-Winter) as well as, the regulation of the day's length! How so?

The four corners of the Earth are connected to the directions north, south, east and west, as well as the fixed signs of the Zodiac associated with these directions. Those cardinal point signs are known as: Scorpio, Taurus, Leo and Aquarius. These "Signs" are also depicted here in Ezekiel as the "Faces" of the four Seraphim before God's Throne, these four fixed Zodiac signs representing all of God's heavenly Creation.

Additionally, these four corners are tied to the four elements: earth (Taurus), air (Aquarius), water (Scorpio) and fire (Leo); the four seasons (circa 4000 BC): spring (Taurus), summer (Leo), autumn (Scorpio), and winter (Aquarius); the four phases of the moon (full, waxing, waning, and new), the four divisions of the day (dusk, midnight, dawn, and noon), and to reiterate, the four major phases of the Sun found at the two equinoxes and solstices every year!

Dear Reader! Can such a preponderance of inter-connected evidence be dismissed as mere conjecture on the part of this author, a cleverly devised scheme to sensationalize the selling of a book? Or, is it just possible that you've embarked on a journey that has been your personal destiny? Can you not feel the spiritual and emotional tugging at your heart as you find more truth pointing you toward a conclusion, an encounter that you've known has been waiting for you all your life? Believe me, I feel it as well!

If such is the case, ours is a straightforward task, provided we understand the heavens as having been Intelligently designed as a geometrical and mathematical apparatus cleverly hidden in the universal form of a Circle, comprised simply of '4 angles' each representing 90 degrees of a 360-degree circumference. Again, you see the '3-6-9's those tonal numbers whose vibrational frequencies are said to be the building blocks of Creation? The empirical data is without argument!

All this evidence is extremely convincing given that Exodus 12 tells us YHVH changed the order, if not the calculation of Israel's calendar: For what purpose? It was necessary in order to enable CONSTRUCTION OF THE CIRCULAR OR DOME TABERNACLE! How so?

Is. 11:12 says YHVH will lift up a banner for the nations and gather the outcasts of Israel and Judah from the 4-corners of the earth. Could these 4-Living Creatures seen in Ezekiel portend this future gathering, its timing, location, etc.?

Let's look back at the Promise to Noah.

**Note: See Gen. 8:22 where he is told:

> *While the earth remaineth, seedtime and harvest, and cold and heat, and summer and winter, and day and night shall not cease.*

The relationship of seedtime and harvest, summer and winter are easily attributable to their calendar positions seen in the equinoxes and the solstices, however, why did YHVH include 'day and night'? Does this not also give us a clue regarding the proper reckoning of His calendar, a cyclical one at that?

Most will stipulate to a hint at the 24-hour day period here. But, is that all? By the way, do you remember He stated in John 11:9, *"...are there not twelve hours in a day? If any man walk in the day, he stumbleth not, because he seeth the light of this world."* What is being said here?

Yes! The 12-hours of day would be literally true during the Spring Equinox where almost equal parts day and night are seen! But, what else is hidden here? To the initiate, Yahshua is the DAY

– The Light – The Sun! It would only be natural for the Day to be divided or parsed out and deposited into 12-hours or disciples, each of whom, would carry the Light into their respective areas!

Mysteriously, all 7 of the Holy Convocations occur during the Solar "DAY" I.E. from Nissan through Tishri. There are 2-festivals: Chanukah and Purim that occur during the Night! Those who keep the 7-festivals will not stumble when you see the darkness because the Light of the World is there. These festivals teach us how to come out of darkness! This is the prophetic fulfillment of John 11:9!

Thus, they/we are birthed out of the Light, becoming children of Light! Ephesians 5:8, 1Thess. 5:5. Further, those disciples, like the 12-Sons of Jacob became a picture of the FACE OF A CLOCK! Each son/tribe is associated with a specific sign, month and breastplate stone. Is it possible then, that our Birth month, Sign and stone have far more influence upon our lives than previously thought? No, you say? Yet, you freely acknowledge that each tribe of Israel and each of the 12-Disciples were individually responsible to impart "Light" into the Body of Messiah!

FACT: Each stone is crystalline in origin, thus it has the ability to record sound (Rocks cry out...) much like a DVD. It can store and release vibrational frequencies, light, sound, and if the human body is crystalline in nature, then perhaps the healing frequencies inherent in the stone peculiar to your Born Month could facilitate energy in the form of: Healing, restoration, stress-emotional relief, etc.

Chapter 6

Not Convinced of A Divine Connection?

Did you know there were tiny microscopic ear crystals deep inside the inner ear called Otoconia that establish balance, equilibrium and motion? Not impressed with the connection?

The Hebrew word for ears is Mozanim, translated "Balance or Scales" and also just 'happens' to be the Name of the Constellation LIBRA, which is associated with the 7th Hebrew Month of Tishrei (And the Fall Festivals of Yom Teruah, Yom Kippur, Sukkot) corresponding to the Daylight of the year which is soon coming to its end.

Incidentally, the planet Venus is connected to Tishrei/Libra and called Nogah in Hebrew, which means 'light'. Its gematria is 58, the same as Ozen – ear (the root of Mozanim) and the Hebrew word Chen translated as grace. This grace is not 'free-unmerited favor', instead, contextually; it indicates the recipient is favored by obedience! Again, BALANCE!

It is important to remember that each of the Holy convocations – those Festivals of YHVH are literally set on the calendar according to the female gestational cycle! Thus, it is on the first day of the 7th-month of the gestational cycle that the fetus' hearing is established! We hear as the vibrational frequencies resonate within the inner ear. Incidentally, from a purely scientific perspective what is heard – its Sound - is literally, light slowed down!

The above number 58 is also the value of Noah who entered the Ark during Libra, Mozanim, and The Scales! The ark thus symbolizing the womb or Tabernacle, the physical dwelling place of the Seed of YHVH!

Additionally, since our focus is on the different increments of time: Yearly, monthly, daily, hourly and so on, it's rather interesting to look at the Hebrew word translated as 'hour' which is only found translated that way in 5 places and all are in the book of Daniel! This word is H#8160, שעה, sha`ah, a moment in time, a look, to regard, to suspend temporarily, to gaze about! How convenient that Daniel was an Astronomer and taught the Chaldeans to observe the Stellar Luminaries in order to bring BALANCE TO THE CALENDAR!

Back to Dividing Day and Night…

> …and YHVH divided the light from the darkness. And YHVH called the light 'Day', and the darkness he called 'Night'. And the evening and the morning were the first day! Genesis 1:4b, 5

This presents a conundrum to many not understanding the Signs in the Heavens and thus we wrestle over when the proposed 'day' begins. Why? Because we fail to notice that the Solar Day as the heavenly pattern, begins as the dark period of the 12th month of Adar ends (Evening) progressing toward the dawning of a new day – month known as Nissan!

Accordingly, following the "evening and the morning" pattern, the Solar Day would end as the Light dims during the 7th month of Tishrei and enters the 3-month period beginning at the autumnal Equinox with darkness settling upon the year during the last 3 months. This fully divides the dark from the day into equal parts of 180 days, 6 months of 30 days! Thus, entirely supporting the evening-to-evening reckoning of Genesis 1!

It is worthwhile to also note the word for 'divided,' as in *"divided the light from the darkness"*. It is H#914, בדל, badal, to make a distinction (Not necessarily a bad one). The root stem Dalet-Lamed can mean that which is weak, emptied out.

Badal has a gematria of 36, the same as OHEL-Tent-Tabernacle, Eleh, to covenant, and which is by chance, another name for YHVH! Nevertheless, the Dalet-Lamed is also the root of a very familiar name: Delilah, H#1807, דלילה, meaning feeble, emptied, dried up. It hints at 'to hang down', to be pendulous, as in a bucket lowered to draw water! It paints a picture of abject thirst needing to be quenched and one found reaching out to do so! This feminine name also indicates to transport!

On the other hand, Dalet-Lamed is also the root of 'Deli' – The Hebrew name for Aquarius, the Water Bearer! As we continue, the prefixed Bet in badal, indicates the House of: Thus, the House of Deli – Aquarius sits between the Dark and Light Periods of the Solar Day at *the evening when one would water the flocks! Just as when Jacob waters the flocks of Rachael!* Though these are the dark months the sun is not absent the house, he is hidden, covered, wombed, waiting to be born again! Hallelujah! Is it possible the dark months are a veil or curtain separating the Holy of Holies from anyone but the Priesthood as in the Tabernacle?

Digging even further into the Genesis text, YHVH calls the darkness "Night", H#3915, ליל, Layil, which comes from the root 'luwl' meaning a staircase, a winding stair, a spiral step, a DNA HELIX! Layil has a value of 70 - the same as the letter Ayin, whose word picture is an eye, a womb, and a well and as such, is also the value of the Hebrew word for secret – Sod. It, Ayin, represents the generations of Israel scattered into the Nations.

Ironically, this word has the same root as the attachment loop of the curtains of the Tabernacle, which would have fit over a dome-shaped, circular construction, forming a DNA Helix where the Manifest Presence of the King would rest! The root hints at a 'folding back', a doubling over in order to form or join two into one! The Tabernacle would have Wombed the Light – which would have been hidden to the outside world!

Just like Noah's ark, and the Zodiacal heavens, as a Tabernacle pattern, the Tent of Meeting would have represented the belly, the womb, the MOUNDED PLACE – רחם, translated rechem, from racham, meaning compassion – mercy. The gematria is 248, the same as Abraham, the Father of Nations. The other word for belly is beten, the hollow mound.

All that being said, we need to address the reality of the matter: The Dark months are not evil; rather, following the message of the gestational cycle depicted in their months, these final 3 dark months are associated with the mystery hidden within the Zodiac's Solar/Lunar feminine menstrual cycle that ends at Nissan, when the day begins! Darkness represents that season of cleansing when the DNA of the Womb is being changed in order that it may become fertile again, insuring that in its cleansed condition it may receive and transport the DNA of the Living Water – the Seed of the Man – Deli – Aquarius! No wonder the True Calendar of YHVH is so vital! Remember, the MAN in Ezekiel's Faces? *More on this later…*

It's also worth noting that Delilah betrays Samson, H#8123, שמשון, the Sun; which is, by the way, the same root as the Middle Candle of the Menorah called the Shamesh or Servant! Rather than betray the purpose of the Darkness, she could have received the Light as his wife. But, that's another story…☺

In View of what we've just seen, the calendar, thus set to begin in the month Nissan or Aviv, coincided with the timing of the Spring Equinox, and coupled with the sunrise and sunset at that time, would have had a far more literal purpose than simply regulating gestational cycles. How so?

Consider this; the Sun's position at this season known as the Spring or Vernal Equinox, would cast shadows on a fixed position in exactly a due east and westerly direction, while the 7th month of Tishrei – Yom Teruah - would reveal a shadow cast due north and south, orienting itself to the Circular Tabernacle design as an eternal COMPASS OR LINE FOR MEASURING! This may pass over your head dear Reader, but may I remind you that Moshe is following the pattern of the first Adam, an eternal role established before the foundation of the world in which, he, Moshe-Adam would serve in the capacity as the Husbandman of the Garden of Appointed Times, condensed and encapsulated within the confines of the Zodiacal blueprint known as: The Tent of Meeting!

Thus, revealing his Priestly role of Timekeeper - Moshe followed the Heavenly Pattern – which would be quite visible if the Tabernacle was indeed set in a Circular fashion, much like a clock face! But, there's even more to the Promises made to Noah!

More Cyclical Confirmation

Genesis 9:12-13 adds even greater emphasis to our cyclical Tabernacle/360-day calendar theory, where as a sign that a flood would never destroy the earth again, we see the establishment of the Rainbow covenant!

It is my opinion that the rainbow, H#7198, קשת, qesheth, bow, an arch, became the emblem set in the heavens for the purpose of replicating the Heavenly Tabernacle Design and thus, setting a pattern for the Wilderness Tabernacle's construction. It's worth noting that the gematria of qesheth equals 800, with 8 being the number of New Beginnings, represented by the letter Chet – as a fence, stairway, helix, boundary, etc.! This may seem odd, since most think of the Rainbow as simply half a circle – Our vision being limited because of the horizon. However, from the atmosphere the rainbow is seen as a FULL COMPLETE CIRCLE called a "Glory" by NASA! *#10

I was dumbfounded upon examining the Hebrew word for rainbow, קשת Qesheth: The letter Qoph is the root of הקפה – haquphah, meaning a circle, to go around, to imitate, to do again! Qoph also represents the yearly and monthly cycles or seasons. The rainbow, thus revealed, clearly demonstrates this eternal cyclical sign given to Noah is a reminder that the Seed of YHVH will be born into a womb of LIGHT, literally becoming the 'Light of the World'!

The letter Qoph also indicates that which comes at the end – that which comes again! This hints at resurrection! The root-stem of Qesheth, the Shin-Tav comes from H#8351-8353, Set, indicating the upper thigh – loins (Hinting at covenanting) it means a foundation, a base, a supporting structure. This root is the basis of the prophetic name of the second Son of Adam, born after the flood, it was symbolic both, of death and resurrection – He replaced Abel. Seth indicates to place, put, to grant in place of, and finally, it also depicts the number 6 the number of Man! It is one of the Creational numbers (3-6-9)!

Therefore, it should not be found coincidental that the Rainbow is strategically, very conspicuous in every instance where these same Living Beings - These Seraphim, which are shown demonstrated in our Wheel within a Wheel discussion are also visibly seen.

Look with me in Revelation 4:6-9 where verse 3 reveals an interesting point: *And he that sat was to look upon Like jasper*

---

* #10. In very rare circumstances it is possible to see a full 360-degree rainbow from an airplane. See photo of one here: https://i.imgur.com/uNaUDVm.jpg

and a sardine stone: and there was a **rainbow round about the throne**, *in sight like unto an emerald.* In fact, Ezekiel, Daniel and John reveal explicit details concerning the eternal throne in the heavens upon which a *"Man"* is seen sitting! In attendance at this rainbow throne are the same surreal Beings, these same Living Creatures! Strangely enough, a rainbow is only seen when water crystals are present and light is refracted through them. The Man – Aquarius, is both that Water and Light!

Consequently, the Sign of the Rainbow ostensibly prophesied that the 360-day calendar year would become the cyclical measure for the seasons. By its very nature becoming the foundation or supporting structure or measuring device from which the covenant could be incrementally revealed, this, in place of another temporary pattern– the previous 364-day, Sabbatical calendar of Enoch!

In doing so, was it possible the Rainbow's most important yet hidden purpose was hinting that perhaps the Tabernacle, which indeed represented the physical blueprint of that covenant, would be circular rather than square or rectangular in construction? And, finally, foretelling that at the end, this sign would once more become prominent as a Calendar measure! Especially pertinent if one calls to mind the words of Messiah in Matthew 24:37:

> *For as it was in the days of Noah, so shall it be in the days of the coming of the Son of Man…*

It should also be pointed out that the Rainbow has 7 primary colors, the Menorah – 7 lights, the festivals, also 7 in number! Coincidence? I think not! The blueprint of creation defies one to separate the significance of these 7's or the 7th-Day Shabbat from the Sacred Cyclical Calendar!

In addition to the Rainbow seen with these Living Beings, as we alter our direction just a smidgen, there are other interesting phenomena that are also revealed in our foundational theme.

Though the KJV translators simplify the text, the SOD or Secret level of interpretation exposes significant supra-natural evidence of a Divine Gateway or Portal that may also account for Ezekiel's transport to the physical location of the Exiles in this story. *Shall we dive into these deeper waters?*

The Whirlwind and the Wheel!

In our first chapter: Ezek. 1:4 Ezekiel describes a whirlwind from the North: [We will discuss this particular location in a short while from now]. The KJV says simply: a whirlwind. However, the Hebrew gives us the phrase: רוח סערה, ruwach sa`arah, translated 'whirlwind'. Oddly enough, this word is seen in Genesis 3 where the Voice arrives in the Cool – Ruach of the day. The word Ruach here can in fact, mean wind, breath, cool, etc. But, it also can indicate a quarter or quadrant as in a specific area of the compass, as in the above whirlwind out of the 'North'.

In historical support of our position here, the ancients divided both day and night into "watches" i.e. 4 divisions of 3 hours. As such the 4th watch of the day occurred around dusk, 6pm, the exact time Yahshua would have appeared as the "Gardener" to Mary after His resurrection!

Strangely enough, the gematria of whirlwind - ruwach sa`arah - is 549, the same as Chag HaMatzot – The Feast of Unleavened Bread - which began on the 15th of the month, the CENTER of the 30-day lunar cycle. The 15th is scientifically proven as the day of optimum ovulation during the feminine menstrual cycle and is also the exact timing during this Hebrew Calendar of the Full Moon. In remarkable fashion as the Creator is want; this would have perfectly matched the timing of the Spring Equinox, the dawning of the yearly DAY!

This is not just any 'Day'! This is the Day of Restitution and

Redemption! The Day Messiah Yahshua went across the boundaries of Physical death into the bowels of the Grave and carried back across that threshold those who had been held captive by death since Adam!

**Note: See Ephesians 4!

This day was a PORTAL to the KINGDOM! Remember when Yahshua told the thief: *"Today you will be with me in Paradise..."* What was He saying? He is revealing how death will be defeated by means of a spiritual transportation superseding the bounds of natural, physical time and space whereby those Captives of Death are led by Him into Spiritual Life and Eternity! There is inherently a masterful, hidden connection here to the vehicle and the Beings attending it, the Wheel Within the Wheel and the Whirlwind – Ruwach ca`arah that transported Elijah into the Spiritual realm that are our subjects in this book!

Peculiarly, alongside the word ruwach is the adjective: סערה - sa`arah, rendered tempest or storm, thus adding a violent emphasis to 'Ruach'. Grammatically, Ruach by itself should have sufficed as a means of describing a simple 'whirlwind'. Oddly though, the Hebrew adds Sa`arah to reveal something extra. For instance, this word can also mean 'rage' and is cognate with Shin-Ayin-Resh, Se`ar, which indicates to divide, cleave, a gate or entrance! This whirlwind shows up when Elijah and Elisha are parted, and it looks as if Yahshua confronts the same anomaly at specific gate in the New Testament - much like He did in Gen. 1 and 3! How so?

Watch what happens in Matt. 8:24:

> *And, behold, there arose a great tempest in the sea, insomuch that the ship was covered with the waves: but he was asleep.*

This was not an ordinary storm, but is described in the Greek as an earthquake: seismos. It comes from the root G#4579, seio, indicating a commotion, a shaking, to vibrate, and to agitate, much as the agitation seen found upon the face of the deep as the Ruach hovered over it in Genesis 1.

To glean understanding, perhaps we should set a backdrop. Initially, we find Yahshua with his 12 disciples upon the Sea of Galilee that body of water which became a reservoir for the waters of the Jordan River whose own headwaters erupted out from under the base of Mt. Hermon at the place known historically, as Banyan, or Panyan, a.k.a. "The Gates of Hell" (Matthew 16:18).

This is the same area where Joshua and the United House of Israel crossed over on dry land while the waters of Jordan were "Cut off" above – to the north from those below! Bizarrely, throughout history this area has been known as a spiritual gateway or PORTAL! Further, following the heavenly pattern we can see the same message in the Southern Constellations, which boast of Eridanus, the river, from whence the root of Yar-Dan is seen. It is upon these waters of Eridanus, that Argo Navis, the ancient ship typifying the Ark of Noah is said to have sailed! Thus, the compass point scripturally known as the 'Sides of the North' seem to hold the key to a dimensional gateway where Spiritual Beings travel. What does this have to do with a probable ROUND TABERNACLE design?

A Circle of Remembrance

If what we've posited thus far bears scrutiny – as Truth should – then our closely held, traditional viewpoint of a rectangular Tabernacle design, with the Tribal alignment around it, as well as, Tabernacle furnishings, and certain Priestly vestments must be examined from this theory of a cyclical/circular – rather than a rectangular design!

We can plumb the depth of the hidden clues, if the reader will first stipulate to any such design being *after the pattern of the heavenlies* as outlined in the beginning of this teaching (Which pattern is indeed, circular) and further, if the Tribal alignment followed that pattern of the Mazzaroth or Zodiacal pattern revealed throughout Scripture and particularly in Job 38:32 (Acknowledged as the oldest of all the books of Scripture) then perhaps a new paradigm is formed!

FYI...

Mazzaroth, from H#4216, מַזָּרָה, defined as the 12 signs (3-6) of the Zodiac, is said to originate from the root, H#5144, נָזַר, nazar, to dedicate, consecrate, separate, to abstain from impurity, and from divine worship, i.e. a Nazarite! Though some may argue, this is the same root of the accusatory word used to describe the SECT of the Nazarenes of which, Yahshua was said to be the leader! Acts. 24:5. Some say the name originated because it had to do with the Nazarite vows, while others argue the place He grew up – Nazareth: However, Nazar is cognate with Nazar and nezer, translated as to guard, keep, observe and branch as in Is. 11:1. Oddly though...

The Jewish Talmud, although it names 63 Galilean towns, says nothing regarding a Nazareth. Nor does any rabbinic literature. There is no mention of Nazareth in Roman records, or any other. Where then does Nazareth originate? It is probable that Nazareth was not on Earth. The sect named Nazarene was derived from a surprising yet familiar source – the Mazzaroth - that also can be translated as Nazaroth-Nazareth! Further, the term 'zodiac' is translated "The Way" and as such, it's message of redemption consistent with Yahshua being referred to as "The Way"!

Both Gesenius and Fuerst translate Mazzaroth as the 12 signs. Both agree to its root: Nazar. Linguistically, the Mem, being changed to a Nun, is allowable in Hebrew. *#11 Nazar as a verb means to encircle. Based on what seems a concerted effort at intentional misdirection, our research, in conjunction with Gesenius and Fuerst as well, reveals that Nazareth and Mazzaroth both mean the same thing!

From these facts, we may conclude that Yahshua was the Son of the Mazzaroth, from the Mazzaroth! Not Nazareth! Thus, when you hear Jesus of Nazareth, it should be interpreted Yahshua son of the Mazzaroth!

Finally, Yahshua's most famous speech is what we call "The Lord's Prayer"! Take note of this: *Thy Kingdom come and your will be done on earth as it is in heaven...*He had to have been referencing the Redemption Plan or Pattern in the Heavenlies and making a plea that it's restoration or completion would hasten! This allows for a more plausible explanation that: *He was called a Nazarene because He followed, kept, observed the Mazzaroth or Zodiacal Cyclical 360-day calendar*!

Another interesting parallel can be seen when we examine this Hebrew word Nezer a little bit further – נזר – in particular Strong's H#5145, which describes the word as 'crown'. It is noteworthy, that the Ark of the Covenant, Noah's Ark and the Table of Shewbread had an intricate wood molding adorning their tops in a 'crown-like' fashion. Additionally, the High Priest wore a turban or diadem called the Nezer or Crown with the words "Holy Unto YHVH" emblazoned on it!

Lastly, Yahshua had a nezer or crown of thorns placed upon His head by the Roman soldiers in a mocking fashion of His claim to the throne of Israel! Each of these are emblematic of the Pattern of the Stars wherein the Zodiac "Crowns" the heavens as a memorial forever of the High Priest of Creation who was crowned King of the Earth even before its foundations were lain!

---

* #11. *Historic Magazine and Notes and Queries*, Volume 23, 1905, pg. 130.

Hallelujah!

The Priestly vestments are just as intriguing, especially armed with the knowledge of Yahshua as our High Priest! Our primary example is that of the Breastplate or Chosen, which is by itself most noteworthy and as such, it is my opinion, that it also (Being adorned with the 12 stones representing the 12 Tribes, 12 Months, 12 Constellations) would of necessity, have had to conform to the Circular rather than square or rectangular designs most are familiar with! Please look at the illustration of another possible design for the Priestly Breastplate below! *#12

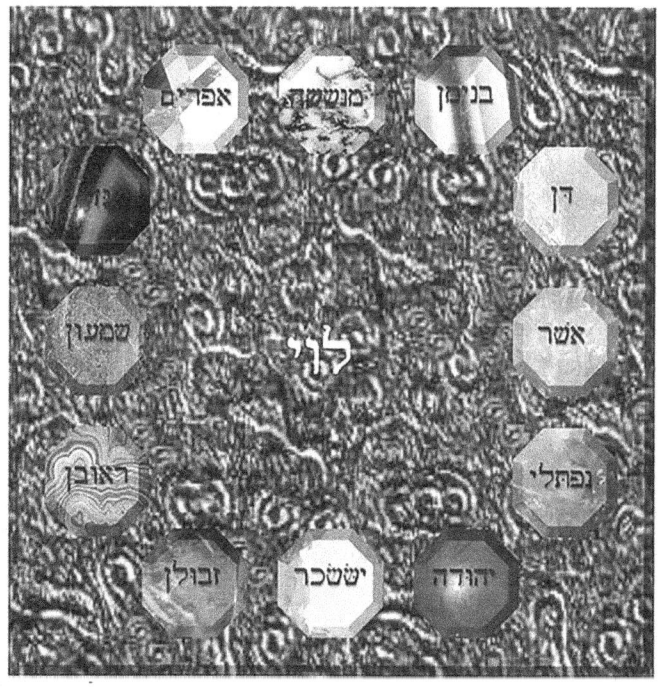

---

* #12. Jewish High Priest Breastplate image is in the Public Domain and is used herein without malice.
https://commons.wikimedia.org/wiki/File:Breastplate(3).jpg

Following our thoughts, after the flood, Noah would himself have been the Cohen haGadol or High Priest of the earth. Therefore if he is given the Rainbow as a token, H#226, אות, owth, sign, mark, to consent or agree, it is my opinion the Choshen-Breastplate's design and orientation would perhaps look something like the above pendant with the 7-primary colors and fastened around the neck while resting upon the Breast of the High Priest! Again, simply put, the rainbow would have adorned the heavens as a multi-colored diadem, nezer or 'crown'.

Against this backdrop, the breastplate or H#2833, חשן, choshen, just happens to have the same numeric value – 358 – as the Hebrew words for Messiah, the root which originates from Mashiach, משיח to anoint, or to draw the hand over. This is quite interesting because the 2-letter root stem, Mem-Shin hints at: The utterance of a prophet, that which flows! Ergo, the Breastplate with its fellows the Urim and Thummim were said to be the source of divine oracles instructing both the Priest and Israel!

Interestingly enough, the Hebrew letters of choshen when rearranged also give us נחש, Nachash, translated serpent. The KJV translation has conjured pictures of a 'Reptilian-like' entity standing upon his feet, when in actuality, the only relationship of Nachash to that picture comes because of the serpent's supposed hissing sound; as the root of Nachash is associated with secretly whispered, magical incantations, enchantments, and the observing of signs. As a result of the corruption of this word it serves to obfuscate the true identity of the ancient Sign depicted in Job 26:13 which speaks as a reference to the serpent or dragon constellation – Drago in the Northern hemisphere!

Let's take a short aside here for a moment:

In keeping with the central theme of a Circular Zodiacal Pattern used as the Template for the Genesis Creation, it seems that Gan Eden would have been the central location, a nucleus or hub, much like the Holiest of Holies in the Wilderness Tabernacle from which the Presence of the King of Creation - YHVH in the Flesh - would sit upon and rule! His throne being depicted: As in Heaven so on the earth! Is this place simply a mythical, ethereal place conjured from the minds of the author of Genesis in order to facilitate the whimsical longings of the weak-minded religious quest seeker as some 'realists' purpose? Or, was it, is it the location of the Throne -Altar of YHVH and His Regent – Yahshua on the earth whose whereabouts have been hidden until just such a time as this?

Chapter 7

Where is Eden Today? Does it Exist?

The truthful explanation of its Kingly venue has befuddled the scholars for millennia. Is there a plausible explanation? If inheritance by right of transfer passes through the First Born who holds allodia title to real property and whatever rests on it, then I find it rather fascinating that the only physical land purchased by Abraham was that of the Cave of Macpelah! Could this be precedent setting case law regarding our inheritance of Eden? Regarding Abraham, *There are no other properties revealed as specifically purchased.* This simple parcel entitled him to an eternal inheritance of this area only with an added stipulation inserted which was shown to include all the trees that were in the field of Ephron, H#6085, עפרון. What then is to be our conclusion as potential heirs of Abraham?

Is there a hidden clue buried (Pun intended) in this text that may have eternal influence upon you and I regarding Eden as potentially, the inheritance promised to Abraham's Seed? Look here at Galatians 3:16 regarding this 'Seed':

> *Now to Abraham and his seed were the promises made. He saith not, And to seeds, as of many; but as of one, And to thy seed, which is Christ.*

There seems here, a specific reference to Messiah Yahshua as firstborn of Abraham's Seed, and to those, who would by faith, accept the redemptive work of Messiah, thereby, allowing them as heirs according to the Promise! Yet, why this one specific parcel of ground? Perhaps a nod toward the root stem of the word Ephron is due? Note the root: Ayin-Pey-Resh, which gives us the Hebrew word aphar – dust.

**Note the relation to Gen. 3:14,19 that tells us man will return to dust and Satan will consume the dust.

Looking a bit deeper, the name of the Cave - Macpelah begins to add a sharper focus to the picture. Do you recall the word picture of the prefixed Mem? It indicates the source of origin, a womb. This leaves us with the primary root of Kaphal, which argues this location as a place where something will duplicate, be repeated, done again. Is it possible that Abraham knew this location by inspiration of the Ruach or Spirit, to have been none other than the gate to Eden where those who had been dust, would return again in the resurrection? It is rather curious isn't it that Adam, Eve, Abraham, Sarah, Isaac and Rebecca, Jacob and Leah are all buried here?

There is no coincidence that even the Rabbis believe this Cave of Macpelah to have also been the gate to Eden! *#13

Furthermore, the Hebrew word for grave is kever, which can also indicate a uterus or womb; thus, as such the grave can become a gate, portal, or connection; providing the one who controls that gateway, the one who has the keys of death, hell and the grave can be overcame! This is exactly the pattern fulfilled by Messiah's 3 days in Sheol!

Consequently, it is highly probable that Golgotha – the Place of the CROWN – not skull – could be the location of the Throne of Heaven once situated in Gan Eden! Since the Garden of Eden

---

* #13. See *Soncino Zohar, Bereshith,* Section 1, Page 57b, 127a.

was created as the Womb of the world, perhaps as Yahshua fulfilled that same blueprint destroying the works of death, His redemptive works at this location will eternally serve as the Womb or Side/Rib for those who return to Adam the Etz Chaim – The Tree of Life – The Living Torah! This would be a Deed of Trust of sorts! Efforts to control this portal or gateway, would lend credence to 'possessing the gates of our enemies'!

Could this have been the literal interpretation, a prophetic partial fulfillment of Isaiah 14:13? *For thou hast said in thine heart, I will ascend into heaven, I will exalt my throne above the stars of God: I will sit also upon the mount of the congregation, in the sides of the north:* No wonder Satan has sought to usurp this throne and thus sit in the Place of Adam/Yahshua!

Moreover, it is this Nachash who represents Lucifer and who is clearly stated to have once resided in Eden the Garden of YHVH and who also wore a Priestly breastplate that only contained 9 of the 12 stones of the Adamic Priestly Chosen-Breastplate! Ezekiel 28:13.

It is also rather apropos here that this Nachash, The Dragon, a.k.a. Drago or Lucifer, is said to have drawn a 1/3 part of the stars of heaven with his tail and cast them to the earth. In view of our study of the 12 Houses of the Zodiac it is more likely that this is in reference to 1/3 of the 12 houses. 1/3 written in decimal form is .33, and 12 x .33 = 3.96! There go those living numbers again!

At present, Drago entwines the North Star or Polaris, the star most fixed at the North polar axis of the earth. However, because of the precession of the equinox the north celestial pole moves in a counter-clockwise manner over a 26,000-year cycle. As a result, another star in the Constellation Drago – Thuban – would have held the Pole-star position – from Genesis until the Polar shift of Messiah's day!

Since Gan Eden the Garden of Cyclical Appointed Times would have been created after the pattern of the heavens, it is highly probable that the center of Eden – like the celestial Fixed North – with its two Fixed stars only slightly apart, Thuban and Polaris, would also see these 2 Polar constants represented by the Two Trees in the midst of Eden – The Tree of the Knowledge of Good and Evil and the Tree of Life!

It is not a random occurrence that the Tabernacle Menorah represented the Tree of Life, and thus though its actual position in the rectangular Temple is argued (*Talmud Menahot 98b*) - based on the more accurate Circular pattern of the heavens and the Polestar location, I believe it would have stood in the north of the Tabernacle, while the Shulchan with its 12 loaves stood to the south, and on the west, the altar of incense. Why?

If we study the Zodiac, when the Sun is said to be "in" a certain sign it means that it actually occupies the opposite sign and casts its long rays of light into the sign shown transverse of it. For instance, if said to be in Gemini, the Sun is actually physically in Sagittarius and *casting its light* into Gemini! The Menorah – The Niyr – Lamp – Light – Sun of YHVH would have occupied the North and cast its light into the South!

In contradistinction with the Tree of Life, the Tabernacle Menorah and Polaris, we find the Tree of the Knowledge of Good and Evil, and Thuban, as Pole Star - would have "controlled" the heavens from the Fall of Adam forward until the time of Messiah, at which time, the ecliptic rotated slightly causing Thuban to lose control! Fulfilling Isaiah 14:13 mentioned above. In Hebrew Thuban is called 'The Subtle', a stark reminder of Genesis 3:1. Could you venture a guess as to when Thuban or the Subtle One lost control? It would have been at the transition of the House of Aries to that of Pisces at the time of Messiah's coming!

The Subtle Serpent

The constellation, Draco derives its name from the Greek, rendered *'trodden on'* as in the Septuagint of Psalm 91:13– *"The dragon shalt thou trample under foot,"* trample, from the Hebrew *Derach, to tread*. In the Zodiac of Denderah Drago is called *Herfent, the serpent accursed!* The brightest star of the latter one's coils is named *Thuban* (Hebrew, *the subtle*) the Genesis fallen Pole Star.

The next star, in the head is called by the Hebrew name Rastaban, *the head of the subtle* (serpent). In the Arabic it is Al Waid, *he who is to be destroyed*. The next star in progression is Ethanin, (also in the head), called *the long serpent, or dragon*. The Hebrew names of other stars are Grumian, *the subtle*, Giansar, *the punished enemy*. Other Arabic names are Al Dib, *the reptile*; El Athik, *the fraudful*; El Asieh, *the bowed down*. You see, even the heavens declare the handiwork of YHVH! Psalm 19:1:

> *The heavens declare the glory of God; and the firmament sheweth his handywork.*

Likewise, we see further confirmation in the prophetic declaration of Genesis 3:15:

> *And I will put enmity between thee and the woman, and between thy seed and her seed; it shall bruise thy head, and thou shalt bruise his heel.*

This is powerfully demonstrated in the Greek depicted constellation Hercules where one foot lies upon the head of Draco. During its yearly course circumnavigating the North Pole it changes to the opposite pictured above!
Back to the Breastplate…

The Choshen is described as a 'pouch-like' vestment festooned with Stones, with the Urim and Thummim inserted inside התמים-

אֶת־הָאוּרִים ואת (Ex. 28:30) Et h'urim V'Et h'thumim. This is translated as: Alef-Tav the lights (revelations) and Alef-Tav the perfections, complete Truth, that which is finished. The letter Hey prefixed indicates that which is revealed. Therefore, this phrase could say: *the Lights reveal The Alef-Tav and they reveal finished Truth!*

Remember, these two oracular devises are inserted inside the Circular Choshen or Breastplate!

The Round Priestly Breastplate.

Since we've been discussing the hidden location of Eden it does seem that clues should abound for those who have ears to hear with! Each of the individual connections already made lend abundant testimony to the role of the physical patterns and the types or shadows they purvey. Moreover, it is the purpose of this work to unravel the mystique that surrounds the divinely inspired vision of Ezekiel, especially as it pertains in great depth to the restoration of incremental facets of the latter day Living Stones Tabernacle!

A fresh look at the visions of Ezekiel, in particular the Wheel Within the Wheel discloses how rife they are with prophetic insight in many realms. We've discussed their relation to the 360-day calendar, the Round Tabernacle, Noah's Ark, The Round Breastplate and other connections. But, we must ask ourselves: "What purpose does each have and how will they affect our future?" Could the role of the individual who served, as High Priest – One who is eternally linked to each of the above, also be demonstrated even more powerfully in a collective or 'BODILY' ministry conferred upon an outcast Remnant out of the House of Israel by Messiah?

Will the revelation of the above Wheel coincide with the release of a Divine Mandate to those who are seeking the Truth while simultaneously exposing the fanatical push toward construction of the 3rd Temple? A Temple which will not be ROUND as its pattern was.

Could this release also unveil the fallacy of the Gregorian calendar that is not Abba's timepiece? Last, but, surely never the least, will we be shown the Manifestation, Release and Identification of the true PRIESTHOOD as opposed to the influence of the Romanish, Edomite counterfeit system upon which, the Whore of Babylon will ride?

These are epic, chilling revelations and will violently expose the chasm between opposing views and challenge us like no other season in history. Each of these deserves its own consideration, yet, in keeping with our text I want to zero in on the possibility of a True Remnant Priesthood hidden within the framework of the revelation given Ezekiel's Wheel – in order to see how it will help reveal their identity!

That being said, before we get too far, I want to stress that it is my opinion Lucifer would have been the First High Priest of both realms: Heaven and Earth! Perhaps a closer look here will bring perspective. In order to sustain our position we contend the following two well-known texts; Isaiah 14 and Ezekiel 28 speak toward this former Being who evidently held this lofty position prior to his exile. Ezekiel 28:13-19 describes his created status Spiritually and Physically as 'Perfect'.

**Note verse 15:

> *Thou wast perfect in thy ways from the day that thou wast created, till iniquity was found in thee.*

The Law of First reference (the occasion of a word's first usage) reveals a connection to his having been perfect – H#8549, תמים, tamiym, at his creation (Tav being Covenant - a mark, and he,

"The marked one"; while Mem-Yod-Mem is the word for water) and as such, the condition of his Perfect Creation is inextricably connected to the controversial events found in Genesis 1:1,2. Where we literally find the Covenant Upon The Waters!

Here, in Genesis the contrast between a Perfect Creation and its later desolate and wasted description is seen. Both Hebrew words tamiym-perfect and Bara'-created - indicate the subsequent Tohu V'bohu – Waste and Desolate condition of verse 2 occurred after the events revealed in Ezekiel 28 which can only be described created perfection and are arguably, thus linked to the allegorical demise of this "Fallen One"!

By the way, Mayim has a gematria of 90, the same as H#3199, יכין, Jachin, to stand firm, be established. This is also the name of one of the columns standing before Solomon's temple facing east. The other being Boaz. These 2 columns point back to the 2 trees within the Garden, and the 2-Pole stars of our previous conversation, each vying for control over entrance into the Cyclical Doorway of the Heavenly Realm! The number 90 is also the value of Melek – King and H#642, אפדה, `ephuddah, the feminine form of ephod or breastplate.

As an aside, it is interesting to note that the Hebrew word Bara' can also point toward something polished, or made smooth, which innocuously connects us to the stones of the Choshen. Ironically, in the original Hebrew text of both Isaiah 14 and Ezekiel 28, the Person named as wearing the breastplate – and referred to in the KJV as 'Lucifer' is not seen. On the other hand, in Ezekiel 28 the "King of Tyrus" is allegorically used as a reference. This Hebrew word for Tyrus is H#6865, צור, a rock or stone, further, it can also indicate to show hostility, to be an adversary. Could Tyrus-Lucifer have become the ENEMY of the Polished Stones – The LIVING STONES UPON THE CHOSHEN OF ADAM? These same stones who would represent the SEED of Abraham through the 12 tribes/sons of Israel? This Round Necklace, like the Rainbow, the Tabernacle, and the 360-

day calendar, was the eternal SEAL of YHVH upon His Remnant Priesthood Seed and the Promise to restore them to Gan Eden!

**Note the following…

Isaiah 14 uses the Hebrew word H#1966, הילל, Heylel, in the sense of brightness, rendered *"Light-Bearer"*, after which the KJV supplies "Lucifer". Curiously the name of the Levitical High Priest, Aaron, H#175, אהרון, is somewhat similar, being translated *"Light-Bringer"*. The Hebrew language reveals a powerful, yet subtle difference between Bearer and Bringer!

This is where things get interesting! The root of Heylel, is from halal, to praise vocally, to speak with confidence, it indicates the condition prior to their individual fall where Heylel and Adam and Chavah (Eve) could literally procreate – without the limitations of the current flesh - by speaking the WORD of Elohiym thus, bringing offspring instantly into existence! Could this same power be inherently connected to the Message of the Choshen-Breastplate? In particular as we consider the Urim and Thummim – The Lights which reveal Finished Truth!

Conversely, the root of Aaron, which comes from haron, the condition of being pregnant, i.e. carrying, bringing, incubating the Seed, indicates an *after-the-fall*, physiological change whereby the WORD or SEED is released into the womb and endures a 9-month gestational cycle before being born! This seems to hint again at Genesis 1 and the Covenant upon the Waters!

Hold on to your seats! Everyone acknowledges that Aaron's breastplate held 12 stones, representing the 12 Months, 12 Zodiac Houses, 12 Sons of Israel. Yet, Ezekiel 28:13 describes the Chosen/Breastplate of Tyrus, Heylel as containing only 9 of those!

Let's stop and think here: 12 stones, 12 months equals 360 days

(12x30) – 9 stones, 9 months equals 270 days (9x30) a difference of 3 months or 90 days. 270 is the value of הסהר, HaSohar (Remember the Bayit HaSohar – Round house?) and נכר, nakar, meaning to recognize or to fail to recognize, to hide one's identity, to fool, a disaster or calamity, to be a foreigner or stranger! Could there be a unilateral effort to befuddle the Truth Seeker with the absence of these stones? Look here:

270 days equals 9 months, the gestational cycle of the Woman! It is she who has the Womb of Water. That womb dwells in darkness, which awaits the Zera or Seed of Light! Zera, H#2233, זרע, has a gematria of 277, the same as H#5828, עזר, `Ezer, as in 'Ezer K'negdo' the Help Meet! Heylel, Adam and Chavah, had the 9 Stones prior to the Fall enabling them to procreate by simply Speaking His WORD and watching the Signs-SONS would follow!

This phrase 'Ezer K'negdo' literally means the One Who is Conspicuously Round In Front – I.E. Visibly Pregnant – In Order To Declare, Tell, Publish, To Make The Seed Manifest In Front! This puts a new spin on Mark 16:17a-20:

> *And these signs shall follow them that believe… and they went forth, and preached everywhere, the Lord working with them, and confirming the word with signs following. Amen.*

Is it plausible that the 'Signs' should more aptly be in front of or by the side of those who preach the Gospel? Much like Eve – Chavah, whose pregnancy indicates the Seed that is planted within her all the while demonstrating the ability to bring to delivery a Son of YHVH!

The Greek Root of the word for 'follow' above (G#190) comes from a copulative form indicating 'to walk the same road'. It is cognate with Alpha (Aleph) and Keleuthos (The Road) If we walk the Aleph's Road – Way, the Zodiac or Cyclical Pathway our UNION with Him will result in our being IMPREGNATED or ROUND IN FRONT! Quite honestly, doesn't a Round Tabernacle, which simply represents the dwelling place of His Seed, seem more suitable as a pattern than the conventional Square or Rectangular model?

We can conclude then, that after the Fall, their physiology, effectuated by their Tohu V'bohu, waste and desolate condition required the need of a physical Union for procreation! This forced YHVH to clothe them with Skins – The Same as the Round Tabernacle - כתנות עור – Kethoneth Owr - Coats of Skins. The gematria of this phrase is 1152, the same as: היתה תהו ובהו והארץ Veh'arets hayitah tohu v'bohu! And the earth was without form and void:

In reflection, is it possible that the extra 3 stones have to do with the vibrational frequencies necessary for the sustaining of life outside the Edenic Circle?

Could Heylel - Lucifer's real intent have been one in which he purposed to prevent the Remnant from returning to that Round House – The original Ohel Mo'ed? In other words, the enemy seeks to hide your true identity and the identity of the ROUND HOUSE – OHEL MO`ED - so that you cannot avail yourself of the miraculous, instantaneous manifestation of YHVH's spoken Word! If so, you will not see signs in front or beside you. This seems to explain the famine of the miraculous that has been ours for generations! Abba Restore Your People!

Perhaps a look at the gematria of 360, the number of degrees in a Circle, the Calendar, etc. would add clarity? It happens to be the value of H#4900, מסך, masak, mesek, meaning to prolong, to delay, to pull someone out of a specific location, it can indicate a price, a value acquisition, a container for seed, a bag. This word masak is cognately related to Masaq, the word rendered Steward and root of Damascus discussed early on! It means birthright son!

Let's Take Another Departure Here…

The Hebrew word Masak/Mesek is first seen in Genesis 37:28 describing how Joseph the Dreamer, has his initial prophetic dream whereby he inadvertently shares with his brothers only to endure what surely must have looked to become like a scattered, prolonged, deferred, postponed, not to be sown - nightmare – particularly after he had been thrown into a Cistern, the dry, round pit!

Incidentally, I call it the DREAM OF THE WAY - the literal pattern in the heavenlies regarding the future of THE PRIESTLY REMNANT OF the House of JOSEPH! Yet, Notice the puzzling hint that can only be found in the Hand of YHVH, as Joseph is depicted being cast within this round pit!

This could not have simply been an evil scheme being developed against Joseph, because after his preliminary deliverance at the hand of Midian, he is later prophetically thrown for the second time-future time - into another pit – this time the ROUND HOUSE OF THE KING AND MADE ITS KEEPER! Remember, he had only just been shown the Message of the Stellar Luminaries, the Heavenly Tabernacle that he arrogantly revealed before its time - to his brothers! What, pray tell is being shown us?

Inarguably, Joseph's name: H#3130, יוסף Yoceph, literally means, "I will do it Again". It's gematria – 156 – the same as Ezekiel's! Again, a divine connection to this misunderstood and often maligned ancient prophet! Therefore, from the time of the Exile of Joseph until his Remnant Seed inherit the Promise, there is one full Circle or Revolution.

A "Do it Again" fulfillment! A full-Cycle! Ezekiel seemed to know something about this, because of His Wheel within a Wheel encounter. *The wagon wheel travels 3.14159, or pi times it's diameter to complete one revolution.* The circumference of a circle – 360 degrees can be found by multiplying radius x PI!

Incidentally, this first round, dry pit or Cistern was situated at Dothan, H#1886, דתן, translated as "Two Wells". The 2-letter root stem being: Dalet-Tav meaning law or edict and is related to da`at, knowledge. By adding the suffixed 'Nun' it diminishes the root. In other words, diminished knowledge.

What happened in the interim between Joseph being thrown into the first round pit – by his brothers I might add - and the second pit? Here's a clue: Dothan has a value of 454, the same as H#2368, חותם, chotham, a seal or seal-ring worn as a necklace upon the breast! This word means to seal up, set a seal upon, to shut, complete, to make an end, close up!

Again, the cyclical comparison underscores that YHVH had His seal upon Joseph even in times of trouble! I'm reminded of Jeremiah 29:11 *For I know the thoughts that I think towards you, saith the LORD, thoughts of peace, and not of evil, to give you an expected end.* Just ask the Prodigal son who himself returns and completes the cycle effectually portraying the reunion of the Whole House of Israel!

It seems the message of the Zodiac was given to Joseph yet, his brothers attempt to circumvent and prolong the Message of the Dreamer and to be honest, Joseph's second time in the pit, seems to follow the same path – excepting the message was secreted away until the appointed time to set the King's Prisoners free! Every Seed has its gestational cycle or appointed time. Galatians 6: 9 *And let us not be weary in well doing: for in due season we shall reap, if we faint not.* The Greek word used for 'due' is G#2398, idios, and indicates *one's own season* or gestational cycle! What may mature season for me, may take a different time frame for you! Don't rush the Hand – Prophetic nudge – of YHVH!

I don't want to be hasty here but, if Joseph is initially thrown into the first pit of (Dothan-Dathan - Diminished Knowledge) out of jealousy by his brothers, is it possible that those same *BROTHERS* were/are now complicit in throwing Joseph into HIS CURRENT pit of religious ignorance and helping to keep him/YOU remaining there? Fast-forward into the future and ask yourself if the Brothers are still attempting to keep Joseph in ignorance of His Birthright and Priesthood! Then answer me!

Chapter 8

A Closer Look into the Breastplate Stones Worn by This Heylel Being...

Two verses in Ezekiel 28:13,14 bear a bit more scrutiny in order to understand the Original design and importance of the Priestly Choshen or Breastplate:

> *Thou hast been in Eden the garden of God; every precious stone was thy covering, the sardius, topaz, and the diamond, the beryl, the onyx, and the jasper, the sapphire, the emerald, and the carbuncle, and gold: the workmanship of thy tabrets and of thy pipes was prepared in thee in the day that thou wast created. Thou art the anointed cherub that covereth; and I have set thee so: thou wast upon the holy mountain of God; thou hast walked up and down in the midst of the stones of fire.*

For the purpose of our study, I want to look at them in reverse order. Verse 14: There are several key words to examine.

- Cherub: H#3742 כרוב

    Rendered angelic being, guardian of Eden. In fact, many scholars agree this same class of "Beings" would have been seen accompanying the Wheel Within A Wheel of

Ezekiel's vision. Not coincidentally, its gematria of 228 is the same as Etz Chayim – Tree of Life; which we also know as The Eternal Menorah or Light of Heaven. This is the eternal pattern of Eden, which HaSatan attempts to counterfeit.

- Covereth: H#5526   סכך   *Sakak*

To fence in, shut in, and encircle, to cover, protect or defend. It is the root of Sukkah or Sukkot! Again, we have the picture of the Cyclical – Round Tabernacle of Intimate Appointments!

- Walked: H#1980   הלך   *Halak*

To walk, to be conversant with, in. To exercise, follow, to and fro. Halak has a gematria of 55, the same as the word Kallah, to hold, contain, restrain, destroy, waste. Yet, it can hint at to be stable, firm, a bride or spouse.

- Stones: H#68   אבן   *Eben*

Stones, from H#1129, banah, to begin to build, as in a family name, to produce offspring, repair, build again, to erect a house. It implies the stone used as a plummet for dimensions, etc. Eben has the same gematria (53) as Gan – garden and Oholibah – "My Tent-Tabernacle in her"!

- Fire: H#784   אש   `*Esh*

Has a value of 301, the gematria of Menorah – the eternal Flame or Lamp of YHVH!

Collectively, we may extrapolate a definition from each of these Hebrew words and add them together supplying us with a hidden

Ezekiel's Wheel Within A Wheel

explanation of Heylel Ben Shachar – Lucifer, Son of the Morning!

It seems the original Office of Heylel was that of protecting, defending the Priestly Role of the BRIDE while the Eternal Flame – SEED whom YHVH planted in Her would begin to build the Kingdom of Priests – The House or Living Stones Tent/Tabernacle! His pride led him otherwise!

Verse 13 gives specific details of the 9 stones adorning Heylel's breastplate. For reference, the Choshen of Aaron has 3 conspicuous additional stones not seen here. The 9 listed in Ezek. 28 are: Sardius, topaz, diamond, beryl, onyx, jasper, sapphire, emerald, carbuncle; additionally gold is added. Zahav H#2091, זהב, that which shimmers, to be oiled, glisten. Curiously, it has the same numeric value -14 as Chagag; to celebrate the cyclical Festivals, to whirl or dance in circles.

Gold is not a 'stone' it is the setting, I.E. the fixture upon which the stone(s) are contained! Thus, representing the cyclical Festivals which, like the Zodiac or Round Tabernacle, becomes fixture upon which the 12 Stones, 12 Tribes/Months/Signs rest! Most scholars arrange the breastplate stones in a rectangular fashion in 4 rows of 3 stones similar to the following: with the third row containing the missing stones of Heylel-Lucifer.

*#14.

---

* #14. Breastplate on the front of the central Sephardic synagogue in Ramat Gan, courtesy of Dr. Avishai Teicher Pikiwiki Israel, source:
https://commons.wikimedia.org/wiki/File:PikiWiki_Israel_34561_Breastplate _on_the_front_of_the_central_Sephardic.JPG

If, as we contend, that the Choshen or Breastplate was in fact, Circular in design, the stones' arrangement would have represented the face of a clock: 1,2,3,4 etc. with stones 7,8,9 missing. The Following is debated, but most Scholars agree the 3-additional (7,8,9 order) stones of Aaron's Choshen are:

Jacinth: Yahweh's **Name** and authority – the tribe of Gad. Possibly Turquoise Blue similar to Tekelet, the Blue Fringe colors. Agate: the tribe of Asher – to restore **life**, to return to Yahweh to do *Teshuvah*. Possibly Gray. Amethyst: To join closely, or to have **unity** – the tribe of Issachar. Possibly Purple. *#15

Let's Look at Their Hebrew Names

1. Jacinth: Possibly ligure (Exodus 28:19) H#3958, לשם. The root is uncertain. However, the Lamed means toward, like, for: while Shin-Mem, Shem is name. It has a gematria of 370 equal to Ayin-Shin – Esh, that is, incidentally, the name of the Great Bear sign – Ursa Major constellation containing the Big Dipper and Polaris the Pole Star!

2. Agate: H#7618, שבו, shebuw, it is related to shavah, captive, to take or lead away. It hints at fragmenting, broken in pieces, a flame. The Shin-Bet root means to return.

3. Amethyst, H#306, אחלמה, `achlamah, shares the root with H#2492, חָלַם chalam, to bind firmly, restore health, be strong, to dream, hence its common name as 'dream stone'. It's gematria is 84, like that of Yadah, to know, to have intimacy with and damam, to be silent, struck dumb, to be destroyed. Its Chet-Lamed root hints at defamation, to profane. Is it possible that this specific stone relates to Issachar's ability to discern the times in order that Israel would know what to do?

---

* #15. Color Source: *Midrash (Bamidbar Rabbah 2:7).*

Joel 2:28 says:

> *And it shall come to pass afterward, that I will pour out my spirit upon all flesh; and your sons and your daughters shall prophesy, your **old men** shall **dream dreams**, your young men shall see visions:*

The phrase 'old men shall dream dreams' in Hebrew is **Zaqen Chalam Chalowm**. Zaqen, normally rendered as 'Old', actually means bearded, mature, an elder who is bearded like a lion! Chalam means to bind firmly, in order to restore to health the prophetic!

Is it possible that these 3-additional stones point the wearer towards the restoration of the Name-Shem and its prophetic connection to the Redemption of the Remnant? This of course, implies a regeneration of the SEED-LINE, a return to the DNA of EDEN that can only be accomplished by also reorienting the Calendar, thus restoring the Understanding of the Way-The Zodiac – revealing TESHUVAH – HOW TO RETURN to intimacy, rather than the fragmented, broken way of the Captive Bride whose womb (MEM) was profaned – chalal!

Why the Breastplate Stones are Important? The Rocks Cry Out?

It is an established fact that certain rocks are crystalline in nature producing vibrational energy sometimes referred to as the Piezo Electric Effect. This relates to the electrical dielectric charges in quartz crystals that when stimulated by mechanical pressure or alternating electrical voltages cause the crystal to vibrate. Its effect is readily known and seen in such areas as: Television, radio, mobile phones and medical equipment such as ultra-sound diagnostics and therapies.

The crystals both transmit and receive! Ironically one method for sending or receiving frequencies is to ENGRAVE THE CRYSTAL, much like a phonograph record, C/D's, DVD's, etc. Hence, the importance of engraving each breastplate stone with specific Hebrew letters-musical notes-numbers-electrical current!

**Note: See Jeremiah 31:31-33.

The Torah will be written in our hearts! Written, H#3789, כתב, kathab, has a gematria of 422, the same as עם ישב Am Yashav, the People Return!

Let's Examine the 3 Stones

- Amethyst: These beneficial effects of this stone are proven in treating various forms of hypertension (anxiety, panic) and hypotension (depression, chronic fatigue). Further, Amethyst derives its color from Manganese deposits. This trace mineral helps in formation of bone, connective tissue, blood clotting, sex hormones, metabolism, thyroid function, and blood glucose levels and neutralizes free radicals. Deficiency results in: heart ailments, blood pressure issues, muscular contraction, bone malformation, poor eyesight, hearing loss, memory loss, infertility, osteoporosis, and much more! Amethysts are said to protect the wearer against "negative" energies, reducing stress, fear and producing SHALOM, tranquility.

- Agate: Though they have some of the same healing properties as amethysts, agates are said to help alleviate bitterness and promote forgiveness, thereby helping eliminate emotional pain, generating a sense of freedom and of being refreshed, renewed.

  It is said they bring grounding and stability. Comprised of

Silicon Dioxide, a mineral which aids the body in detoxification (Perhaps removing that bitterness mentioned above?) It alkalizes the body neutralizing the acidity that promotes all disease. It heals, restores, hair, nails, teeth, promotes wound healing and regenerates skin, while also reducing plaque accumulation in the arteries and restores the mucosa in the respiratory tract.

- Jacinth: Said to instill wisdom, this stone is a barometer of health, its luster fading as health deteriorates. Its color is disputed but, based on the correlation to the Greek description in Revelation 9 it seems more likely to have been the ancient Carbuncle, a.k.a. 'anthrax' due to its glowing ember - red streak color. It is thought to protect against plague, wounds and injuries and promotes spiritual growth.

Curiously, the 200 million army of Revelation 9:17 are said to wear breastplates of fire, Jacinth and brimstone. Many Critics will pooh-pooh this information as irrelevant, Pagan or New Age in origin; yet, the same narrow minds employ their use on a daily basis in cell-phone and other electronic devices! Which devices have the proven ability to emit EMF waves in powerful forms, that can alter DNA, kill plants, insects, humans, they are without doubt, currently being used in warfare technology.

The devices using these frequencies can modulate and manipulate weather, mimic the human voice, understand it, and frankly the same technology is being used in the Hadron Collider which many scientific opinions believe has already opened the Spiritual Portals around the earth and yet in this discussion the antagonists argue their original source, the crystalline stones themselves, have no useful place in the Believing Community? You make the call!

It is therefore no accident in my opinion, that we see Messiah making a powerful reference to the Crystalline Stones crying out as seen in Luke 19:36-40. Here, the text reveals the triumphant entry of Yahshua into Jerusalem amid the clamorous adulation of His disciples and others in attendance, whereupon, the Pharisees immediately solicit Him to silence and rebuke the offenders. Yahshua then makes this statement:

And he answered and said unto them, I tell you that, if these should hold their peace, the stones would immediately cry out.

The timing of this event is advantageous to our position having occurred during the Traditional parading of the Lamb before the People in preparation for the Blood Atonement sacrifice for the Nation. The Levites would line either side of the street and wait for the signal of the High Priests' approach in order to break into Praise and Worship at the entrance of the Lamb! In the greatest 'photo bomb' ever, Yahshua came in from the opposite direction and stole their thunder! Literally fulfilling the message, that we believe to have been inherently *written in the Crystalline DNA of the three-MISSING breastplate STONES!*

FYI - Anias and Caiaphas led these Levites: These prominent figures in 'Religious' history are held in infamy by most who regard them as mostly responsible for the execution of Messiah. What most don't realize is the depth of their influence upon the Priestly Order and the deception that is rampant even today among adherents to the restoration of the Levitical Order! It is an established fact that neither of the two named were of true lineal descent in regard to the Kohanim or Aaronic order. Rather, in collusion with the Roman government they literally bought the position! For those who question my claim, I submit the legally entitled High Priest was none other than John the Baptist, whose father was murdered in an effort to subvert the priestly line!

This gives reasonable credence explaining the People flocking to John's baptism and the fact that the Messiah Himself, by submitting to the same, openly legitimized John as the High Priest! Now Dear Reader, you understand the following statement found in John 3:30 *He must increase, but I must decrease.* John knows there is no Ark of the Covenant in the Temple, a charade perpetrated upon the House of Israel to this day! He also knows that the Levitical Priestly Order must decrease to ensure that the Melchizedec Priesthood with Yahshua as the eternal High Priest be allowed to function as it was designed in perpetuity from the origin of the Creation pattern!

What follows, as we delve into the Prophetic nature of the names or Shem of the counterfeit priests, only solidifies our position regarding the significant influence the design of the Breastplate, the order of its stones, the cyclical calendar, the Round Tabernacle and Ezekiel's confirming vision of the Wheel within the Wheel, all have on our current understanding of 'End-Time' eschatology!

Those bogus priestly contemporaries of John the Baptist have names defined respectively as Anias – YHVH has favored and Caiaphas – The Comely Stone! These two, as ANTI-MESSIAH FIGURES – purchased the coveted role of the High Priest from the Roman government, and were found masquerading jointly as the COMELY STONE WHOM YHVH WOULD FAVOR! THE FOUNDATIONAL STONE OF MESSIAH!

I contend, the restoration of the Breast Plate stones points toward the Revealing of the Lamb, Yahshua – The Word of YHVH – Now deposited into and found clothing the Remnant Kings and Priests! Those, whose sole mission or purpose when read in Luke 4:18,19 (Isaiah 61) seems to follow the same healing pattern in the frequencies of these 3 stones! Moreover, I believe a powerful unveiling of the role and person of the Anti-Messiah will also coincide with the future disclosure of this information!

Before we go further, could the term "Revealing the Lamb" be akin to having the DNA of the Creator inseminated into the Womb of the physical, spiritual, mental and perhaps cyclical TABERNACLE OF THE BRIDE who has been TOHU V'BOHU

FOR 2 Days, 2,000 years? Hosea 6:2 gives us an exciting point of view:

> *After two days will he revive us: in the third day he will raise us up, and we shall live in his sight.*

The phrase: *"After two days"* – יחיינו מימים ביום Yihchenu M'yomiym B'yowm has a gematria of 282 and that value is seen in a phrase found in Genesis 1: 10 taking place *after the 2nd Day* – where we see the waters being gathered - ולמקוה המים uwl Miqveh h'mayim: Which is translated: At The gathering together of the Waters! Miqveh, from qavah, means ordering activities around an expected future event! It indicates a line for measuring as in Psalms 19:4 where we find the eternal timekeeper – The Sun – vividly depicted traveling upon the measuring line of the Stellar Luminaries or Zodiacal Heavens!

The word for waters is Mayim – Mem-Yod-Mem: The letter Mem which brackets the Yod, indicates chaos or: **a Womb with the YOD or SEED of YHVH deposited in it**"! This is a powerful prophetic shadow picture first visible here in Genesis 1:10 connecting us to the Future Prophecy of Hosea 6 and the coming 3rd Day! As in the Genesis account, in spite of the enemy's plans the waters are no longer found Tohu V'bohu – waste and desolate - in the 3rd day! We are living in that 3rd day NOW! This is the DAY OF THE LATTER RAIN - THE MIQVEH OF LIVING WATERS! It is no accident that Yahshua exited His Wilderness journey on the 10th of Tishri – Yom Kippur – The Day of the Wedding Miqveh! As prophesied, here are His Promised Vows to His Bride!

> *The Spirit of YHVH is upon me, because he hath anointed me to preach the gospel to the poor; he hath sent me to heal the brokenhearted, to preach deliverance to the captives, and recovering of sight to the blind, to set at liberty them that are bruised, to preach the acceptable year – Yovel or Jubilee of YHVH.*

In light of the above you should be able to see the reason we believe the Breastplate and each of the other cyclical accoutrements, including that of the Round Tabernacle are being restored to prominence! What is more, you can see the importance of these 3 missing stones if we add the combined value of their Hebrew names: Leshem, Shebuw, Achlamah = 762. From this we get the value of the phrase: תשבני, Teshvehni – You Shall Not Return and עצמות יוסף, Etzmoth Yoseph – Bones of Joseph!

It is also the value of:

ולהבדיל בין האור ובין החשך

Uwlhavdil bein h`owr uvein h`choshek:
And to divide the light from the darkness!

This phrase is seen in Genesis 1:18 where the stellar luminaries are set in the heavens to divide light from darkness! This is an intriguing statement! Did you know that it is a repeat of Genesis 1:4 where Elohiym speaks light into being and segregates it from darkness? With one difference, from this time forward, it is the stellar luminaries who serve as אות – owth, signs, proof, That, Which (He) who is to come – They remind us of Torah, The Word, who from now forward will divide Light From Darkness! Owth has a value of 401, the same as ישעיהו, Yeshayahu, Isaiah – YHVH IS SALVATION! It is the Salvation – Redemption Plan of YHVH – Messiah in the FLESH that separates light from darkness!

Erroneously, the focus has been on this division of Light from Darkness! Can division be good? What actually happened was a new 'forming' out of a formless - Tohu creation and a new 'infilling' out of an empty - Bohu one! AND ELOHIYM SAW THAT IT WAS GOOD – H#2895, טוב, most often rendered 'good', yet, it hints at being fertile, ready to receive seed. What was good? THE WORD BECAME FLESH IN A TOHU V'BOHU BODY! Yahshua came in the form of the Adam whose fleshly body had death working in it! Thus, for all intents and purposes, Adam's body – our body – was/is a waste and desolate vessel! That is, until Messiah took on Himself that same flesh, without sin, which is the contagion, the vehicle death works through! Notice the pattern throughout the Wilderness Tabernacle System:

It is an established fact: None of the Tabernacle rituals; whether the daily sin offerings, the Yom Kippur National atonement or the Red Heifer purging, were meant as an eternal means of expunging personal or National sin! Rather, each only 'Postponed' the debt lawfully – extending mercy - until such time as the penalty for sin could be completely satisfied. James 1: 15 stipulates that *sin when it is brought to maturity – (I.E. The Note is due) it brings forth death.*

Remember this! The reintroduction of DEATH to the Body of Adam brought with it the insertion of the hybridized Seed of the Nachash through the now opened spiritual doorway into the natural realm – Genesis 3! There are consequences for eating, dwelling at the wrong Altar-Tabernacle!

How? Each of these rituals represented a temporary sin penalty remedy for THE MAN, because after Adam - no man had yet been perfect who could die for himself! Adam would have had to remain without any blemish to complete the Pattern! AND IF HE HAD, THERE WOULD HAVE BEEN NO NEED FOR ANIMAL SACRIFICE!

Ironically, after the gathering of the Waters YHVH declares for the first time: It was good - כי-טוב, ki-Tov; Tov's gematria – 17 – is the same as חוג, huwg, a circle, a vault specifically a circular horizon. To inscribe or build into a circle! Is it possible that YHVH – Elohiym separated Seed here - from the Womb – Darkness - much like in Genesis 1:28 'Male and Female created

He 'them' only to separate 'them' and form and fill 'them'? This puts 'Divide' into a different perspective...Let's look. Is it possible that Heylel – Lucifer, by himself, did not have the ability to procreate while the Tohu V'bohu condition existed? Prior to the Fall, did Heylel, Adam, and Chavah have the ability to speak word into flesh, producing and procreating without the need of a male-female physical body? Can the Missing Breastplate Stones, which reveal and restore the EDENIC – DNA also reveal and restore that Power? You Make the Call!

Pay attention to these verses, Matthew 12:43-45:

> *When the unclean spirit is gone out of a man, he walketh through dry places, seeking* **rest***, and findeth none. Then he saith, I will return into my house from whence I came out; and when he is come, he findeth it* **empty***, swept, and* **garnished***. Then goeth he, and* **taketh** *with himself seven other spirits more wicked than himself, and they enter in and dwell there: and the last state of that man is worse than the first. Even so shall it be also unto this wicked generation.*

The highlighted words are from their Greek roots and indicate: #1. To be at leisure, a vacant office, to possess in the sense of wearing. #2. To draw or drag, as in before the judge. To choose by vote. #3. To set in proper order, adorn, garnish. It is used with the ornament or arrangement of the Stars also to order a government or a constitution. To receive, obtain, to care for.

Look at this definition! As you do, you'll see why Yahshua the Messiah, had the power over demonic and fallen-angelic principalities! He never abdicated His Throne or Office, though He took on a lower form in Adam's flesh! You should also – NEVER – relinquish the Throne of YHVH in your hearts to the fear or lies of the enemy! Look at Adam and Chavah!

Did Adam-Chavah vacate their office, by failing to wear the

Priestly Breastplate, which assured proper order of the Constitution of YHVH they were entrusted to care for? They were afterward-naked H#5903, עירם, eyrom, naked, to be subtle, crafty, to be made bare: Bare or bereft of what? Eyrom's gematria is 320, the same as *Ebeni Nezer, My Consecrated Stones!*

If you recall, nezer can also indicate a throne! Those, Ebeni Nezer could also say My Consecrated Throne! The Tabernacle or Ohel – Tent of YHVH is His throne in you!

Further, looking back at Genesis 1 and the dividing of light from darkness we see the Hebrew word for Divide is H#914, בדל, badal; meaning to make a distinction, *especially from things previously mixed though, not necessarily in a bad way!* The gematria is 36, the same as Ohel – Tent – Tabernacle!

36 is also the value of אלה, Eleh, to covenant with, to make a sworn oath, a Constitution – the word picture is that of a terebinth or long-lived memorial tree. Tree in Hebrew is a keystone word, first seen in the Original Creation account. Euphemistically, it represents man in general and Messiah, as the Tree of Life, in particular. It is written H#6086, עץ, `ets, from `atsah, which can mean to close the eyes, to shut the door, and it also hints at knowledge, advice, a plan, a backbone! If we're not careful we'll shut our eyes, closing the door to the backbone of the Cyclical Plan of Redemption typified in the Round Heavens, Round Tabernacle, and Round Breastplate!

Curiously, the word Eleh is also the root of אלהים, Elohiym! Again, this is interesting because Darkness is first seen in Genesis 1:2 'upon the face of the deep' at the same time the Ruach Elohiym is seen hovering upon the face of the waters: Tehowm – translated deep versus Mayim – translated as waters. It is here that Creation is first called: *Tohu V'Bohu* being rendered: Without form (Tohu) and Void (Bohu).

In a wry twist, the Hebrew language reveals that Tehowm – deep, has the same root as תהו, Tohu – without form – the first usage of which connects us to days 1-3 of creation where the Waters, Light, Day, Night, Land, Seas, etc. were given 'bodily' FORM – afterward, they are then depicted as filled! Much like Genesis 2 where Adam's body is without form - Tohu and Ishah's – the Woman's body is filled after being empty – Bohu!

At this point in the text she is referred to as Ishah, and is not called Eve – Chavah until Genesis 3:20. Chavah means to explain, interpret, from a root stem indicating a riddle or puzzle and also indicating a vault, circle, the circular horizon a tent! After the Fall, death again reigns in the earth and the resultant effect of sin now causes her body to revert back to the Genesis 1 condition of Tohu V'bohu again! Having been apprised of the Redemption Plan of YHVH for Creation since his beginning Adam makes what is essentially, the LAST PROPHETIC CREATIVE DECLARATION of EDEN CALLING HER – Chavah - THE TENT WHO WILL REVEAL THE ANSWER TO THE RIDDLE OF redeeming CREATION!

This is indeed powerful and consistent with the prophetic role of the Stellar Luminaries and the Breastplate Stones, in particular the 3-missing from Heylel's –Lucifer's Choshen, which seem to reveal the pre-existence of and perhaps foreordained information as regards the plans of Elohiym to implement certain redemptive functions which are now (Post Fall) missing in the ADAM. He, who like the Ishah – The Woman – The Bride – has lost his ability to function as The Help Meet – עזר כנגדו, `Ezer k'negdo to YHVH in the earth.

If we do cursory review of this word `Ezer, the Hebrew letter pictures supplement our understanding. Drawing a more complete sketch of what has been a baffling encounter that seemed to have derailed the Creator's plans forcing Him to an alternate plan. Nothing could be further from the truth! Look at the Ayin-Zayin-Resh word pictures:

Ayin indicates a well, womb or repository, while Zayin-Resh means seed. Ezer's root hints at girding, a surrounding. The Kaf prefix speaks of like, as, toward; While neged speaks of that which is in front, in the sight of, before the eyes, indicating a mirror image.

Each individual letter's illustration points at a form needing to be filled, a BOHU - a womb prepared with Seed, whom the Host would gird, surround and protect that seed while becoming the Mirror Image of the One Whom She Stands Before! The Bet-Hey root forms a personal pronoun indicating 'In Her'. The suffixed Vav means 'mine', his, belonging to HIM! Bohu has a value of 13 – the same as Echad – If we are not Echad with Him we are in a waste and desolate condition! תהו ובהו, Tohu V'bohu a phrase whose value is 430, relating to the years of Exile!

In support of this claim, it's remarkably fascinating that our study of Ezekiel mentions in chapter 23 of the parabolic existence of two daughters. This text reveals 2 women who committed whoredoms in their youth: Samaria-Ephraim known as Aholah, H#170, אהלה, translated as 'Her Tent' and Jerusalem- called Oholiybah, H#172, אהליהבה, 'My Tent In Her'.

With Ohel being the root, the verbal form אהל, ('ahal) appears to have described the forming [out of Tohu] of an intended and artificial communal core for the explicit purpose of exchanging dialogue and forming language and cultural expressions. Derived from the noun אהל, ('ohel) describes a place where minds merge. [A filling of what previously was empty -Bohu]

Interestingly, Heylel and Ohel, both have the same root letters: It seems we've lost the Tent of His Meeting – The Round Tabernacle of His Presence in our midst replacing it with a shining counterfeit, no longer capable of speaking His word into flesh! Lucifer-Heylel, surely confirmed that role!

Therefore, it is no wonder that the gematria of the phrase 'Help

Meet' used a few paragraphs earlier to describe Adam and his Wife – The gematria of the Hebrew rendering 'Ezer k'negdo is 360! In order to complete that role, the Woman was separated – Badal – from the ADAM – the Light; she represented the Darkness, the Womb, who must be filled by the Zera – Light! Without the Supernatural Miraculous light frequencies of the 3-missing stones, whom do we resemble? WHO DO WE PROCREATE AFTER – WHO IS IN OUR TENT - Heylel or Yahshua the TRUE LIGHT?

Chapter 9

The Hidden Keys: Alef & Tav!

It is our contention that the High Priests' Choshen or Breastplate would have been a cyclical, Tabernacle shaped pendant worn upon the breast. Festooned with the 12-Born Day Stones of each tribe together with the letters associated with their names. This 'necklace' could very well have provided an elaborate light display as each word spoken from YHVH creates a vibrational frequency that is transferred to those same individual letters. As they are illuminated in turn, the message is literally written upon the Heart of the High Priest! This adds new meaning to Jeremiah 31:33:

> But this shall be the covenant that I will make with the house of Israel; After those days, saith the LORD, **I will put my law in their inward parts**, and **write** it in their **hearts**; and will be their God, and they shall be my people.

Let's delve a bit into the Language of Truth and see what's hidden there! The highlighted words in Hebrew above read: נתתי את-תורתי, natati ET-Torahti. I will set, ascribe, utter, and assign the Aleph-Tav - My Torah, in their H#7130, קרב, qerev, midst, hearts, literally in their middle! I will write, H#3789, כתב, kathav, write, record, inscribe, engrave upon their hearts, H#3820, לב, lev, heart, [from a form of lavav] so that they become intelligent, regarding what is written - that which encircles, encloses them!

YHVH will write the Torah upon our breasts causing us to understand; to gain intelligence regarding what has been written (above and upon us) that which encircles us! Is it possible as Priests of Elohiym that upon our breasts/hearts will be written the Pure Language – which I believe to be Hebrew - as a Choshen of sorts much like this proto-type? Does this sound far-fetched? Perhaps, but you've heard it before, only didn't understand what you were looking at! First, let me remind you that both the Ark of the Covenant and the Ark of Noah were facsimiles of ADAM – I.E. The Man with the Torah – The Remnant Seed of YHVH in him!

**Note: Gen. 6:16:

> *A window shalt thou make to the ark, and in a cubit shalt thou finish it above; and the door of the ark shalt thou set in the side thereof; with lower, second, and third stories shalt thou make it.*

This word for window here is another curiosity. It is used 24 times in the Old Testament and only translated 'window' this one time! The writer of Genesis knew the power inherent in the Hebrew language and though the KJV translators failed to follow suit, as we uncover the truth we can see that this was no ordinary 'window'.

The word used here is H#6672, צהר, Zohar; rendered elsewhere as 'light', noon, and a double light, specifically, the sun! In addition, whatever this device is - it serves as a channel through which the light is refracted! Zohar can also indicate splendor, a shining, to glisten like oil! What is more, Zohar has a gematria of 295, the same as *Yeriyah*, a word used to describe the Wilderness tent housing the Ark before the Temple is built: 2Samuel 7:2.

Now, here's where your paradigm either shifts or grounds to a halt! Is it possible, in keeping with the Circular Heavenly Pattern – after which the ROUND Wilderness Tabernacle was constructed – that perhaps Noah's Ark could also have been fashioned in a circular design as well? Remember YHVH is consistent and orderly! He does not change! Could Our Traditional concept of the Ark's Design be Wrong? Please pay attention to Genesis 6:15:

And this is the fashion, which thou shalt make it of: The **length** *of the* **ark** *shall be* **three hundred** *cubits, the breadth of it fifty cubits, and the height of it thirty cubits.*

The highlighted words did not exist in the original text. So, let's examine a few very controversial Hebrew words in **Bold text**.

- Length: H#753   ארך   `Orek

  Rendered 'length' as in linear here. However, the majority of the instances it's used it indicates *an element of time*! To prolong one's days, to survive after, to postpone or defer anger, to lengthen one's cords, as in a tent.

- Ark: H#8392   תבה   *Tevah*

  Defined as a basket or chest. It has the same gematria as Alef-Vav-Tav – Owth, a sign, and monument, a token.

- Three: H#7969   שלש   *Shalowsh*

  Translates to. 'three'. However, please note the gematria – 630, the same as H#3747, keriyth, hollowed or dug out – a separation, cutting (circumcision?)! 630 is also the value of Seraphim the Living Creatures at the center of our Teaching!

- Hundred: H#3967   מאה   Me'ah

    Rendered 'hundred(s)'. Now, here's where a curious thing happens! Me'ah has the same letters as Cubit – Alef-Mem-Hey, Emmah. The stem here comes from the root 'em – mother! It also hints at the threshold as in covenant, the beginning, head or foundation of something!

Without going much farther, it seems more than mere constructional dimensions are implied here! Perhaps I'll be accused of twisting words to fit my narrative, but these hidden words are here nonetheless! You be the judge of this extrapolated definition!

This Ark becomes a picture of the BELLY OF THE MOTHER – a hollowed out place, where for a season, it's occupant(s) are protected, as a monument or Tent-Tabernacle - where multitudes – me'ah, hundreds of hundreds will be birthed!

Do You Require Secular/Scientific Confirmation?

British Museum Curator Irving Finkel describes an ancient 4000-year-old cuneiform tablet discovered giving explicit details of a circular vessel with a 220-foot diameter and 20-foot high sides. *#16 It gives precise details of materials, the 'two-by-two' loading of animals! The dimensions describe an area of 3.6 sq. kilometers (2.2 miles), a base approximately 38,750 sq. feet!

If constructed in a dome-type shape, a roof or top covering would

---

* #16. Reference: "Ancient Tablet Suggests Noah's Ark Was Round" by Associated Press, *New York Post*, Jan. 24, 2014. Source: *http://nypost.com/2014/01/24/4000-year-old-tablet-suggests-noahs-ark-was-round/*

be simplistic to add, and in fact the ancient cuneiform text mentions the occupants going "up on the roof" to pray! Therefore, could the window described in Gen. 6:16 have actually been an aperture at the top of the vessel, much like the dome-shaped Tabernacle allowing the Sun to shine inside the vessel, consequently giving Noah specific compass readings, and a calendar in order to calibrate his time inside and to reorient him for when the waters dried up - according to the fixed Stellar/Solar positions based on the info conveyed in the Zodiacal Living Creatures? You make the Call!

*#17.

Further, could this Window have been a portal of sorts into a Spiritual dimension? Could Noah have communicated with YHVH in some fashion through whatever vibrational frequencies of light that were allowed to enter the vessel by way of the Portal or 'Window'?

---

* #17. Noah's Ark Illustration © Mashosh, shutterstock.com
Source: https://www.shutterstock.com/image-illustration/noahs-ark-illustration-767091028

Perhaps Noah was receiving much more than just rudimentary compass points for navigational direction? It is quite possible! He was the first Mariner! Could the Creator through this Gateway have provided him information, verbal messages, and specific dates and times that He and the other occupants of the Ark might schedule a divine encounter, a Visit of sorts? If, as we've suggested, Light passed through this gateway or portal, couldn't that light also have been artistically created to represent the Presence of the Creator or His Word – The Alef – Tav – and presented as the Urim and Thummim upon the Breastplate of the High Priest who himself would be a microcosmic Ark?

All the more, in support of our position, it is almost universally agreed the Hebrew Language is cyclical in its nature! Remarkably, having just said that, the word for Hebrew is Ivrit, which has a gematria of 682, the same as the phrase: בית הסהר bayit HaSohar - The Round House! Doesn't this sound a bit like the window in the Ark – the Zohar - A round window of light? Frankly speaking, the overwhelming amount of presumptive evidence cannot be the result of random coincidence! The mathematical probability alone makes our perspective one not easily dismissed!

Another point in fact, which only increases the merits of our analysis is that the phrase Bayit HaSohar is, not surprisingly, the name of the dungeon or prison where Joseph was kept in Egypt! Genesis 39:20,22. Take a look with me at verse 22:

> ...and the chief of the round-house giveth into the hand of Joseph all the prisoners who are in the round-house, and of all that they are doing there, he hath been doer;

The prophetic significance of the Outcasts of Israel being currently gathered from among the nations and even more so, that many Jewish authorities admit, though not always accepting, these 'Strangers' as the House of Joseph or Ephraim is staggering! In keeping with the pattern of his life, Joseph has been sold into bondage and at a future time of great world upheaval, he must, of necessity rise to a position of prominence, which will thrust him quickly into a powerful office where he can begin implementing the plans for the survival of the Whole House of Jacob! The Nations – including his Brothers – will be humbled in a fashion that will enable Joseph to present himself – with conclusive evidence that he is indeed their Savior, Redeemer typified in the Person of Messiah! The Sages teach that while in Egypt the method of confirmation used by Joseph was to Speak to them the Language of Torah – Hebrew and to present his own mark of Circumcision! I believe he also reaffirmed his right as First born and High Priest of the family! It's hard to argue such a point when you're the one in a humbled position!

Od Yosef Chai – Joseph Lives!

Who is Joseph today? Has he been in the prison of spiritual Egypt? Is he about to be delivered and then favored? Will this Joseph be in charge of the ROUND HOUSE that is the Tabernacle? HaSar Bayit HaSohar? The Prince of the Round House? Fact: Joseph's faithfulness get's him promoted to 'KEEPER OF THE ROUND HOUSE'! IS THAT PROPHETICAL? While we are preparing to exit Egypt, the House of Joseph is given charge of all those who have been the King's prisoners and he again, is given charge of the Round House! The King's Prisoners -The Melech Asere! Those bound, hitched, yoked, in obligation of an oath, fastened in any sense to the KING! I said "he again is given charge of the Round House" because I firmly believe, having been the First born of Jacob and Rachel, given the Coat of Many colors, that Joseph was, in fact, the High Priest of his family!

Having said that, he would function as a mediator, much like he did while imprisoned. Look at the above Hebrew word for prisoner shown here which is H#615, אסיר, Asere. Its gematria,

271, is the same as mekurah, meaning birth, origin, ancestry and herayon, meaning childbearing, pregnancy. The Round House – Bayit HaSohar is the place of your ancestry – DNA, your birthplace! Seems another confirmation of the Melchizedek Priesthood of Joseph!

Looking back at how scripture remembers him, it surely isn't coincidental that Joseph wore a RAINBOW GARMENT AND DREAMED OF THE 12 HOUSES OF THE ZODIAC! The value of his name – 156 – is the same as OHEL MOED. Tent of the Calendar and Ezekiel!

As we continue, concerning the ancient methods depicting the Hebrew language as being expressed in the cycles – circles of life it baffles me that we can see its affect in the physical, natural world vividly expressed in the seasons, gestational cycles, and Zodiacal heavens, as well as, the Holy Convocations. Isaiah 46:10 states it thus:

> *Declaring the end from the beginning, and from ancient times the things that are not yet done, saying, My counsel shall stand, and I will do all my pleasure:*

The phrase 'end from the beginning' is reminiscent of "I AM THAT I AM" The Alpha and Omega, the Beginning and the End! Each describes a circle of infinity! So what exactly could the Breastplate with it's Urim and Thummim – The Aleph and Tav - have represented if not a foreshadowing of Messiah placing His Tabernacle within Adam who reigns as the first High Priest of the Earth! By the way, it is said that the Alef and Tav – the beginning and the end – are also depicted in the Zodiacal houses of Aries and Bethulah! These two are fittingly portrayed as the Husband and Bride!

Further, the I AM phrase is first seen as a definitive name of the Creator in Exodus 3:14 where in answer to questions regarding the identity of the One Sending him Moshe is told to let Israel know that he is being sent by none other than "I AM THAT I AM" **אהיה אשר אהיה**. While here, take note of the gematria that is, in itself intriguing. The combined value of the doubled Ehyeh – Ehyeh = 42, the same as Emmah, Mother or the Hebrew word for cubit! The middle word Asher – that, which, was, will be, is the root of ISRAEL and means to go straight! This is a word picture of ISRAEL IN THE WOMB OF YHVH! This is the shadow picture of the Round Tabernacle! 42 is also the value of Yovel, **יבל**, the word indicating a Jubilee year or the year of Release! It's not an accident that Moshe is being sent to deliver or Proclaim the Yovel of Israel at the 50th jubilee (a 50-year celebration) 2500 years from creation!

As we continue, were there, as most traditional adherents propose, just 2 of the 22 Hebrew letters within this round Priestly breastplate pouch or is it possible that all 22-Hebrew letters, collectively represented by the Alef-Tav were included? Remember, Scripture clearly states that His word, both individual words and in totality are Light (Urim) and His word is Truth (Thummim)! Ps. 119:105.

Additionally, if the Priests are truly speaking His word as Oracles, then Is. 8:20 emphasizes the same! If you read the following 2 verses, we're being warned of a counterfeit system where it seems the false religious leaders those who are wizards and those with familiar spirits, in their perversion of the Message of the Zodiac will also look to the Stars for answers for themselves…

> *To the law and to the* **testimony***: if they speak not according to this word, it is because there is no light in them. And they shall pass through it, hardly bestead and hungry: and it shall come to pass, that when they shall be hungry, they shall fret themselves, and curse their king and their God, and* **look upward***. And they shall look* **unto the earth***; and behold trouble and darkness, dimness of anguish; and they shall be driven to darkness.*

- Testimony, H#8584   תְּעוּדָה   *Te`uwdah*

    From Ayin-Vav-Dalet, uwd, to return, repeat, surround, go round, encompass!

There's another interesting connection here, first seen in Genesis 2: 6 where a 'mist' is said to have went up from the earth. This word for mist, comes from the root of H#181 אוד, also pronounced 'uwd. The Ayin and the Alef are both silent letters and therefore interchangeable. But, it's the root origin that dumbfounded me! It more aptly refers to a raking together of the blazing embers of a fire! Is this also depicted in the role of the Oracles? Can they also be seen as blazing embers upon the breast of the High Priest?

Exodus 28:30 tells us that while Aaron bore the Urim and Thummim upon his heart that simultaneously, he bore the judgments – Mishpatim – the process or procedure for litigation, exoneration, legal cause, vindication, execution and sentencing also upon his heart. Hinting that the Urim and Thummim rendered that verdict in some fashion!

Another interesting purpose of the Urim and Thummim is found in both the books 'minor' works of Nehemiah and Ezra, leaders instrumental in the return of the Exiles to the Land. In each of these cases a specific leader named תרשתא, Tershatha, (Ezra 2:63, Neh. 7) is found declaring that no exile whose genealogy couldn't be proven may eat of the Most Holy things, until the priest with the Urim and Thummim stands-H#5975 עמד, to stand, arise, appoint, ordain, to cease, stop, be established. By the way, the combined gematria of Nehemiah and Ezra is 391, the same as H#3444, ישועה – do you recognize the True Deliverer or Savior of the Exiles that are now being gathered? Yeshuw`ah!

The word seen above, Tershatha, has the same root letters as Genesis – B'reshiyt. Is it possible that the Urim and Thummim represent the DNA of Creation and as such, when this Most Holy thing is consumed, will offer proof of your DNA and inheritance in Israel? The Most Holy Thing – Manna – Living Word – Torah – Messiah?

Isn't it also interesting that a place existed where the lineage of those entering the Tabernacle was checked against a family registry? We would know it today as Golgotha – infamously known as the place of the skull – which is actually a misnomer! It indicates a skull as in "Head Counting" – the polling place! The root of Golgotha – galal, indicates to roll, that which is round, a circle! Yahshua finished the Work of restoring the Circle of the Heavens, the Calendar, the Round Tabernacle, and the Right of Inheritance at this ROUND PLACE! Could Golgotha be at the gate of Eden?

In addition, the Messiah often referred to as "The Nazarene" though out of ignorance of the true origin of that word! It can be translated as Nazar – a Branch or Crown, and is the more accurate root of Nazaroth – not Mazzaroth! This title connected Yahshua to the Message of the Stellar luminaries those 12-Houses which Crowned – Encircled the Heavens! Oh, in case you're skeptical, this would also have been the location of the Altar where the Red Heifer is sacrificed, call the Miphqad gate.

If you remember Genesis 3: 24 the gate to Eden is called the 'Way' – דרך, Derek, and has the same value as Miphqad – 224. This is the Gate where the heads of families in a type of census are numbered and the Brazen Altar where the Red Heifer was burned! By way of reminder, the word Zodiac means 'The Way'. This helps explain why Yahshua said He was 'The Way'. If all these different links are making since, then the purpose of the vision of Ezekiel and the Wheel within a Wheel could plausibly have served as a historical lynchpin reconnecting past and future. This could, quite conceivably, be a Marker on the Way or Road revealing to Ezekiel and us, the King's Highway, the avenue for return to Eden! I'll let you evaluate the evidence and prayerfully, you'll come to the same conclusion as this poor author! We have stumbled upon a revelatory key to the future restitution of all things as spoken of in Acts 3:21:

> *Whom the heaven must receive until the times of restitution of all things, which God hath spoken by the mouth of all his holy prophets since the world began.*

Let's look back at the phrase in Ezra 2:63: Where the Priest stands up with the Urim and Thummim, specifically, at the root Ayin-Mem-Dalet in the above word amad, to stand; which can indicate a period of time, a duration of time, generations: The Dalet indicates a doorway! Is this hinting that the restoration of the Circular Tent of Meeting, Ohel Mo'ed, Tent of the Calendar of Appointed Times, will present a doorway or portal which will reveal the DNA of those in attendance?

Could this be prophetic of our day and the restoration of the Circular Tabernacle, The 360-day calendar, and the Round Choshen-Breastplate with the Urim and Thummim, the Alef and Tav inside?

Are These Alef and Tav A Viable Missing Puzzle Piece Today?

If you note, the Aleph was originally depicted as an "OX Head". The Ox or Bull associated with Taurus, the Bull and the Individual houses or decans of the tribes of Joseph (Ephraim, Manasseh, Benjamin) properly aligned on the West side of the circular Tabernacle.

This unique latter form - not coincidentally – the children of darkness more often wiser than the children of light - resembles the Masonic compass and square supposedly used by the architect of Solomon's temple, *which we contend as a result would have also been circular in construction*! This information cunningly hidden by the Powers who want to assure we're unable to find our way back to Eden! Further, the Tav takes the form of the 4-cardinal points of the compass in what could simply be described as a 'plus + symbol' or cross-like emblem! Therefore, if we follow a straight angle toward the East we find the House of Judah, connected to the Lion-Leo (Judah, Issachar, Zebulon) ensign!

The orientation of the Alef and Tav could serve as a "Pointer" or Clock Hands - depicting angles or Houses of the Zodiac as well as, the 4-cardinal points of the Compass – North, South, East and West representing the Eagle/Dan/North, The Man/Aquarius/Reuben/South, The Lion/Judah/East, and The Aleph - Ox/Joseph (Ephraim, Manasseh, Benjamin) West! Thus, the Aleph depicts both 45 and 90-degree angles while the Tav includes the circumference of 360 as well as 45 and 90 and 180 degrees! 45+90=135 1+3+5=9. Together, both form a square within a circle, much like DaVinci's Vitruvian man drawing we saw earlier!

Ezekiel's Wheel Within A Wheel

**Note the Aleph and Tav *#18 and the demonic counterfeit *#19, both pictured below!

---

* #18. *The Complete Messianic Aleph Tav Scriptures* by William Sanford, CCB Publishing. Used by Permission.
* #19. Masonic Square and Compasses by Eric Cable is in the Public Domain and is used herein without malice.
https://commons.wikimedia.org/wiki/File:Masonic_SquareCompassesG.svg

Chapter 10

Three Calendars?
360-364-365
Which One Do We Use?

The Earth makes a 360-degree rotation around its axis in relation to the distant stars in one "sidereal day". However, in relation to the sun, due to the earth's orbital movement, it rotates on its axis a bit more than 360° per (solar) day, giving it a 'wobble effect'. This way in 1 year the Earth makes 1 extra rotation in relation to the stars. However, we define our 24-hour "day" relative to the Sun, not relative to the Earth's actual rotation. Thus, it seems the axial relation is out of sync with the 24-hour days comprising the solar 365.24-year.

From our study thus far we can conclude that we've had several calendar changes from Genesis forward and in fact, at least 2 other events not yet mentioned that would have necessitated the same: One is the account of Joshua in which we witness the Sun and Moon standing still and a second much later, counterclockwise miracle that was relative to the miracle of the Sun-dial in Hezekiah's day, the 8th century B.C. Both are well documented in secular history as well as, Biblically! (We simply don't have time to delve into these here)

It is also worth noting, based on Ezekiel's revelation and his obvious connection to both Daniel and the Book of Revelation (which reveals the same Living creatures) and the specific time frames mentioned: 42 months, 1260 days, 3 and ½ years, that a return to the cyclical 360-day calendar seems likely! Again, in my estimation, the above is congruent with every cyclical or round pattern brought to attention in this work! Simply put, a true, round circle would have to be dissected into 360 equal degrees! The number 360 is shown being easily divisible by 12 (Months, Houses, Tribes, Breastplate stones) and 30 (Days) 2 (Alef and Tav forming right angles) and much more.

Likewise, Yahshua remarks in both gospels of Matthew and Mark: "...*except the days be shortened no flesh should be saved...but for the Elect's sake...*" Mt. 24:22, Mk.13: 20. This is in reference to the Noachian 360-day calendar and the emphasis placed upon the subsequent phrase: "As it was in the days of Noah, so shall it be in the days of the coming of the Son of Man". Why would a hint toward the shortening of our current 365.24 calendar year and the likelihood of a return to a 360-day calendar be necessary? Both Disciples answer! *Then if any man shall say unto you, Lo, here is Messiah, or there; believe it not.* Shouldn't that be the ultimate purpose of the Calendar of Appointed Times? To serve as proof of who Messiah is, and whom we are, by how and when we celebrate the Holy Convocations! A counterfeit calendar points toward a false Messiah! What is more, the above texts cite global upheaval, chaos on a scale never known by man! Why wouldn't the King of Creation provide a mechanism by which the entire House of Israel could function in Unison?

We could communicate, travel, worship and much more in a united Body that would provide a powerful witnessing tool, much less, providing a corporate shield of protection and shalom! Oh, never doubt it my Dear Reader that Unified Body celebrating on a worldwide scale in unison is shortly in front of us!

In support of what I believe to be a seminal work, I have presented and sought out, several opinions from sources outside my circle of influence (Pun intended) whose position would not be swayed by my own. Undeniably, there are many extra-Biblical sources that add significant strength to what is surely already a position that is hard to argue against! Yet, the duty is yours. Test what I've shared and Truth will stand on its own merits! I will refer you below to notable excerpts from a well-known, though often ill received book, The Book of Enoch. Ill received and ostracized, I might add simply because of the myopic and opprobrious views of Religious Tradition! What was/is there to hide? Plenty it seems!

Though many may pooh-pooh the validity of the Book of Enoch *#20, it is worth noting that in chapter 80 2-8 Enoch mentions some interesting things that may find merit and perhaps, validate this author's position in the days ahead:

2 And in the days of the sinners the years shall be shortened,
And their seed shall be tardy on their lands and fields, And all things on the earth shall alter, And shall not appear in their time: And the rain shall be kept back And the heaven shall withhold (it).

3 And in those times the fruits of the earth shall be backward, And shall not grow in their time, And the fruits of the trees shall be withheld in their time.

4 And the moon shall alter her order, And not appear at her time.

5 [And in those days the sun shall be seen and he shall journey in the evening on the extremity of the great chariot in the west] And shall shine more brightly than accords with the order of light.

---

* #20. The *Book of Enoch* is in the Public Domain, source: https://book-ofenoch.com/about-us

6 And many chiefs of the stars shall transgress the order (prescribed). And these shall alter their orbits and tasks, And not appear at the seasons prescribed to them.

7 And the whole order of the stars shall be concealed from the sinners, And the thoughts of those on the earth shall err concerning them, [And they shall be altered from all their ways], Yea, they shall err and take them to be gods.

8 And evil shall be multiplied upon them, And punishment shall come upon them So as to destroy all.

It is our contention that Enoch was prophesying to and - about the DAYS OF NOAH and the ensuing, catastrophic Flood, which affected the orbital wobble of the Earth whereby the 364-day year, would revert back to that of a 360-day. This sets into motion the prophetic summation of Yahshua in the Gospels cited below.

If this causes the listener to give pause, doubting the veracity of these statements, Please remember the words of Messiah Yahshua who seems to be directly quoting Enoch or He is at least familiar with his words. Why? Because what He is revealing is the Zodiacal precession of the equinox during its yearly trek! Matthew 24:37 *But as the days of Noah were, so shall also the coming of the* **Son of man** *be.* Who is this 'Son of Man'?

At the time of the appearing of Messiah in the first century at 12/21 at midnight, computer models reveal the winter Solstice the time when the sun is darkest and cannot give up its light. There, the Son of Man – ORION – can be seen descending to the earth! One month later, it disappears. Simultaneous with this annual Winter Solstice, during what is known as the Festival of Hanukah – The Feast of Lights, Yahshua the Light of the World was conceived! Further, 3 days later, after his disappearance in the Zodiacal West, Orion ascends in the East! Typifying the birth, death and resurrection of "The Son of Man"

David Mathews

*#21

The Pattern

The Heavens are, without question the original, eternal pattern of the Tabernacle plans given to Moshe, as well as, the source for calculations of the Hebraic Calendar. What remains hidden and purposely, if I might add, is whether that pattern which is the premise of this book, can be applied to the Wilderness Tabernacle and the Priestly vestments and can they, as such be viewed as a mechanism for Divine Information, Divine appointments, future

---

* #21. "Orion", plate 29 in Urania's Mirror, a set of celestial cards accompanied by *A familiar treatise on astronomy* by Jehoshaphat Aspin, 1825, is in the Public Domain and is used here without malice.
Source: https://commons.wikimedia.org/wiki/File:Sidney_Hall_-_Urania%27s_Mirror_-_Orion_(best_currently_available_version_-_2014).jpg

protection, sustenance, as well as a possible vehicle for inter-dimensional travel, etc.?

Moreover, if such is an eternal, fixed model and the template such that, a 360 degree model is without doubt the 'Witness in the Heavens', then the second witness required by Torah for conviction, corroboration, and attestation as a Covenant document, then that second witness must not deviate from the first or original template! You're argument then, is whether the Wilderness Tabernacle in its schoolmaster role is sufficient enough to be considered a Witness.

If so, given that traditionalists have Moshe's pattern divergent in an overt and deliberate manner from this 360-degree template, having him choosing instead to construct what is plainly an aberration! Yet, this is what is presented conventionally as a Divinely Inspired square or rectangular fabricated Tent of Meeting! My question? Wherein lies their body of proof? Indeed, what legitimacy does it claim as a witness of the heavenly design? The KJV and other traditional religious views have been purposely pointed in the wrong direction in order to accommodate the agenda of those who have usurped the role of PRIESTLY TIME-KEEPERS!

Conversely, if Moshe in fact, followed the Circular Design, then why has it been hidden and what does this mean for the much touted square/rectangular 3rd Temple proposed by the Zionist Movement in Israel? Could they be found aiding and abetting the coming Anti-Messiah and his kingdom; the agenda of which, is such that it strives to impose his dictatorial will in order that he may seek to wear out the Saints!

**Note the word phrase 'wear out' in Daniel 7:25.

- Wear out: H#1080   בלא   *Bela*

    This Bet-Lamed root is seen in Babylon – a word defined as confusion by mixing. It is also the root of the Hebrew word for flood – Mabbuwl – seen in Genesis 6 and again in Revelation 12 where a flood issues out of the Mouth of the Dragon! Bela has a gematria of 33, the same as Gimmel-Lamed, the root of Gilgal, Golgotha, and Galilee – I imagine you've figured by now that it is also connected to our Cyclical Theme as it means a circle, a mound, to roll away! In passing, you must ask: Why would Yahshua choose the place called the 'Circle' – Galilee as a place to begin redemption?

Furthermore, The Hebrew letter Bet in בלא indicates the HOUSE, while Lamed-Alef forms a word meaning NO! In pursuit of their hidden, scurrilous religious agenda, these Soul and Mind Zombies who are stupefied accomplices of the Anti-Messiah will say NO to the Building of the Genuine House of YHVH – The Tabernacle of Living Stones! So, in order to consolidate our facts and tie up the loose ends allow us to continue in our pursuit of the True Tabernacle Pattern – The Wheel Within the Wheel. What better place to start than by examining a few clues beginning with the Wilderness Tabernacle and its *Master builder*: Bezaleel. Exodus 31:2 *See, I have called by name Bezaleel the son of Uri, the son of Hur, of the tribe of Judah:*

- Bezaleel: H#1212   בצלאל

    His name is translated "in the shadow or image of EL". The letter Bet as shown above, hints at a house, specifically a tent. While the root Tzade-Lamed indicates to cover, to hide, darkness, image, and a shadow! The explanation of the name implies his character as one who historically had been revealed to have been found, like the Psalmist, *'Residing in the Secret,* H#5643, סתר, *cether,*

> *place which allows him to abide under the under the Shadow of the Almighty'*. Psalm 91:1. The gematria of cether is 660, the same as H#4701, **מצנפת**, misnepet, which describes the Turban wrapped around the High Priest's head! The Mem prefix indicates origin or womb as in the birthing place. But, notice the root letters: Tzade-Nun-Pey-Tav, if you simply rearrange them to form Tzade-Pey-Nun-Tav, you get the first part of the name given to Joseph by Pharaoh! Tsophnath Pa'neach! The name implies One Whose Head is encircled: One whose Mind is engrossed – physically, like the Stones around Jacob's head as his pillow, like the Circle of the Zodiac, Like the Crown of Thorns upon Messiah's head! The latter part of the name – Pa'neach indicates Pey – the mouth, to speak and Nuwach - Noah – to Rest!

Because of the pattern inspired by the Ruach and placed into the mind of Bezaleel, his thoughts or mind thus, causing his head, his mind to be encircled by the Crown or Turban of the heavenlies, the Pattern of Creation! Bezaleel, like Joseph before him was tasked in his priestly capacity with building the Living Stones Tabernacle according to the eternal pattern as a place of Rest for the Head of Messiah like Jacob, the Father of Joseph who first saw the DNA Helix of creation and placed his own head upon the pillow of these same Foundational Stones! Following this eternal pattern, the Greater Exodus will again see Joseph in his role as the Master Builder of the Living Stones Tabernacle rising out of the exile of Egypt after enduring a season of chaos and once more, promoted because his character will also indicate that he has spent time in the Secret Place of the Most High! Now, look a bit closer at the lineage of Bezaleel…

He is the son of Uri. The Gematria of Bezaleel equals 153 the same as: Beni Elohiym - Sons of Elohiym. Uri, H#221, **אורי**, is rendered 'light', My Light, fire, revelations. It is the root of Urim! It gives direction as in the East where the "Light" arises! Hur, H#2354, **חור**, is poorly translated as "hole", its root means to be white, pale, to be made clear, evident, splendid, noble. A hole, aperture, an eye socket.

The Tent whose image/pattern will reveal the Perfect Light Who Rises (from the East) clear and splendid to the eyes of the Sons of Elohiym! Again, this eternal pattern is written in the heavenlies as the Constellation Orion and depicts the death, burial and resurrection of Messiah! Does this extrapolated definition of his name really matter? It does if the Tabernacle was indeed, circular in design!

Further, if an opening were provided in the top of the tent dome, it would have allowed for the detailed keeping of a minute-by-minute circuit of the Sun through the 360-degree Heavens [Psalm. 19] and a yearly reckoning through the months or houses of the Zodiac as well! Additionally, it would allow for the alignment of the luminaries at fixed points to establish Azimuth and elevation, mathematical angles that provide for exact navigation necessary to determine location in the Wilderness desert!

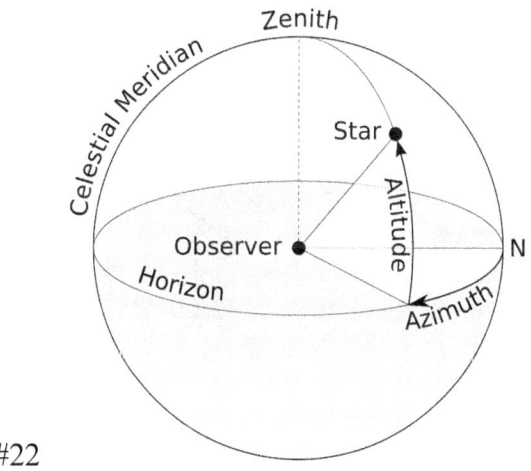

*#22

---

* #22. A schematic diagram of the terms "Azimuth" and "Altitude" as they relate to the viewing of celestial objects, courtesy of TWCarlson. Source: https://commons.wikimedia.org/wiki/File:Azimuth-Altitude_schematic.svg

I found it also intriguing that both the Prophets Amos and Isaiah speak of the future restoration of the Tabernacle of David rather than a 3rd Temple construct. Both use a Hebrew word different from tent-ohel, instead, referring to it as a Sukkah, H#5521, סכה, which interestingly has the value of 85, *the same as the word Ephod*! If you recall, the Ephod would have contained the round 'necklace' of the Chosen/Breastplate. That being said, how can the word Sukkah be used to infer a circular pattern, when it is defined as: a booth or hut? Let's see...

First, Samech is a mystical letter - its ordinal value is 15 (1+5=6) while its gematria is 60 hinting at the sacred numbers 3-6-9 and the 360-degrees of the Circle! The origin of the ancient pictograph is disputed. Some say it had a thorn-like look: If encircled by a fixed ring to describe a 360-degree sextant perhaps it could look like the one below?

*#23

---

* #23. Phoenician letter samekh by Ch1902 is in the Public Domain and is used herein without malice. Source:
https://commons.wikimedia.org/w/index.php?curid=3853286

David Mathews

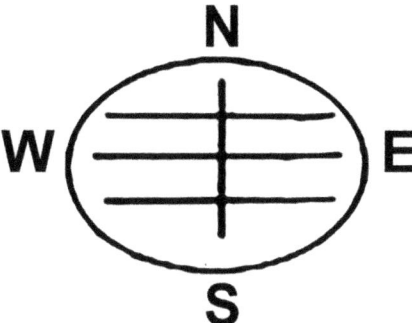

The Samech in the word Sukkah represented the marriage chamber, the intimate place for the cycles of life to be renewed! This is the very purpose of the gestational cycles of the Divine Appointments clearly delineated on the Sacred Calendar inscribed by the Tent of Divine Appointments – Ohel Mo'ed! As noted, The Hebrew word for seasons is *moed*. It means appointed meeting. Its root *yaad* is more revealing in light of the frequent scriptural references to Yahshua's coming being likened to a wedding feast. *Yaad* has within its definitions to appoint for betrothal and/or for marriage.

The Samech much later evolved into its modern circular design. Spiritually, Samech represents a support, a cycle, and a round of years or recurring seasons. It hints at the beginning and the end of a life cycle: Hence, in the ordinal list of the Hebrew Alef-Bet, it follows after the letter NUN – life and in succession does the letter Ayin – The eye, follow the Nun. *To see the cycle of life!* If the Samech is completed circumscribed by a Circle, as in our crude drawing above, we can see the center vertical line could represent North-South, or longitude while the 3-horizontal lines represent a latitudinal east to west orientation: The center being at 0 degrees, the equator and the hemispheres or Poles at 90 degrees!

Therefore, the Fixed Zodiacal Points representing the Spring and Fall equinox and the Summer and Winter Solstice portrayed by the 4 Created Beings who represent the 4-cardinal compass points and the Camping alignment as revealed in our revelation of Ezekiel's Wheel Within a Wheel! The Samech, Vis a Vis the Sukkah, would seemingly play an important role in the foreordained intimate DIVINE APPOINTMENTS of Messiah and His Bride!

Further, in like manner, Messiah Himself – The Light of the World – is conceived during the Festival of Lights that takes place at the Winter Solstice of Dec. 21st – during the Sign of Aquarius – The **Man**/Water bearer. Fulfilling scripture's prophetic message, we would have already watched His cousin, John The Baptist – The Last of the Kohanim – being conceived at the Summer Solstice June 21st – under the Zodiacal Sign of Leo – the **Lion** 6 months previous!

The Moedim or Appointed Festivals follow the same Gestational or Menstrual Cycle! Thus, the Zodiac becomes a celebration of the birth, life, and death of the Sun/Son!

Winter Solstice 3 months/Dark days/New moon/menstruation

Spring Equinox 3 months/Waxing Moon/Pre-ovulation

Summer Solstice 3 months/Full Moon/Ovulation

Fall Equinox 3 months/Waxing Moon/Pre-menstrual

This would put their births at the opposite Points of the Zodiac during the Spring Equinox 1st of Nissan – Sign of Taurus, the **Ox** (John) and Tishri, the Fall Equinox 23rd of Sept. – Sign of Scorpio/**Eagle** (Yahshua). This makes 9 months of 30 days = 270 days from Solstice (Sun Stop) to Equinox (Equal Night) and with a lunar cycle of 30 days the full moon occurring on the 15th resetting the gestational cycle! It is a factual reality that when the Sun is said to be 'in' a specific sign, that it actually is passing through its opposite while shining light into the 'occupied' sign.

This adds additional clarity to what was spoken by John the Baptist in John 3:30 *He must increase, but I must decrease.* John knew that the Light of Messiah's Melchizedec Priesthood would increase while that of the Levitical order would diminish!

Supplemental to that is verse 31 of the same chapter where John describes Yahshua as from above or from 'heaven'. The Greek word used here is G#3772 ouranos, indicating the Sidereal or Stellar luminaries! What is more, ouranos is where the 7th Planet of our solar system gets its name! If this piques your interest, there's yet another amazing connection here as well! On more than one occasion, Yahshua makes a powerful, hidden declaration: *'The Kingdom of heaven, G#3772 ouranos, is at hand!'* Matthew 3:2, 4:17, 10:7.

What could He possibly have intended by such a mysterious dictum? As we've asserted early on, the Zodiacal calendar YEAR is divided into 12 houses or 'month-signs' of approximately 2,160 years! Yahshua arrived on the 4th-day or 4,000th year at the beginning of the Piscean Age! Pisces is symbolized by 2-fish connected by an umbilical cord of sorts. Thus, the 'coincidental' calling of 12 disciples that were fishermen and what has heretofore been an innocuous multiplying of a meal of fish on at least 2 occasions should not surprise those familiar with the Zodiac!

Accordingly, His second coming is timed to coincide with the end of the Piscean Age and the beginning of Aquarius – The Water Bearer! What is not quite as obvious, except to the students of astronomy is that each Sign of the Zodiac is governed or ruled by, the planets! Aquarius is ruled by – you guessed it – URANUS, the 7th planet!

In support of this, many who watched the skies pointed to 1996-1997 as the birthing of Aquarius which was entered into by Uranus for the first time in 77 years in a planetary alignment with 6 other bodies! In January of 1997, those same 6 formed a Grand

Sextile: six planets – 60 degrees apart literally forming a 360 Circular Tabernacle for Uranus – Known by ancients as the God of Heaven - in a prophetical announcement of the "Dawning of the Age of Aquarius!

In ancient mythology Uranus was also called – The Rain Maker – reminiscent of Joel 2:23:

> *Be glad then, ye children of Zion, and rejoice in the LORD your God: for he hath given you the former rain moderately, and he will cause to come down for you the rain, the former rain, and the latter rain in the first month.*

Juxtaposed to the Western mindset or calendar, the latter rain spoke of by the Prophet Joel would have occurred during the spring months of March and April, announcing the Spring Holy Convocations of Pesach and The Feast of Unleavened Bread! This season of outpouring – forgiveness of sin – cannot happen without REPENTANCE! This seems a prophetic declaration of a massive Egypt-like Exodus event that turns the hearts of those affected and causes a revival of a magnitude never seen before! Hallelujah!

At this time a great outpouring of the Spirit of Elohiym will take place as revealed in Zechariah 12:10:

> *And I will pour upon the house of David, and upon the inhabitants of Jerusalem, the spirit of grace and of supplications: and they shall look upon me whom they have pierced, and they shall mourn for him, as one mourneth for his only son, and shall be in bitterness for him, as one that is in bitterness for his firstborn.*

Note that it says: House of David – which I believe to have been referencing the Tent of David a pattern after the Cyclical Heavens. Further, it is said: *"They shall look upon me whom they have pierced"*. This pierced one is Aquarius! Curiously, in the center of this sign is what is known as The Helix (DNA Helix?) NGC 7293, or Caldwell 63 and is a huge planetary nebula in the center of the Constellation Aquarius! It is commonly referred to as "The Eye of God".

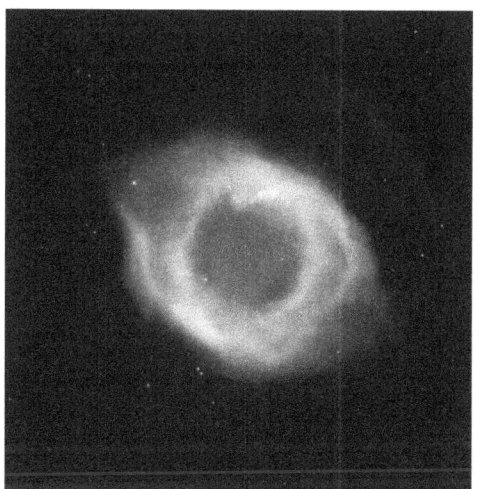

*#24

Frankly, I'm blown away that even in this picture of the dwelling place or Heavenly Tabernacle, a Tent if you will, there seems to be an aperture – opening – an eye in its midst confirming much of what we've shown regarding the cyclical structure of the Tent of Meeting the Ohel Mo'ed! We've quoted from Psalm 91 on several occasions throughout this teaching specifically addressing the secret place of the Most High that affords us protection. Those who choose to not dwell there are subject to the noisome pestilence, H#1698 דבר, pronounced deber; the same root as Dabar – word. A destroying word comes for those opposed to the Secret Place. Ironically, the value of the phrase 'Eye of God' –

---

* #24. The Eye of God (Helix Nebula NGC 7293) by Dylan O'Donnell is in the Public Domain and is used herein without malice. Source: https://commons.wikimedia.org/wiki/File:Helix_Nebula_The_Eye_Of_God_D eography.jpg

עין אלהים, Ayin Elohiym, 216, is the value of the same word used to describe the Holiest of Holies! The center of The Maqowm where the light would enter – the Eye: The eye brings light to the Body!

Chapter 11

Ezekiel's Tabernacle and the Bones of Redemption: Ezekiel 37:1-28

As we continue in the vein of our previous position, where we have stated that we believe the Wilderness Tabernacle to have been designed in a Circular, Round fashion and as we've entertained the Torah through the lens of Ezekiel's Visions - it becomes apparent - this same Physical Tabernacle was created as a temporary illustration, a shadow picture of a much grander *Spiritual* Tabernacle comprised of the Living Stones of the Remnant of Israel!

It is the prophesied "Gathering of these Living Stones" that is the focus of our annual Sukkot (Remember the word Sukkah?) celebration – This is a cyclical yearly Holy convocation where the Unification of the Whole House of Israel – I.E. "Unity In His House" becomes the preeminent objective regardless of whether one is Jew or Gentile! It is this Unity that produces Righteousness – Love – Power! To achieve this lofty position we must understand the PATTERN! We contend that apart from this revelation of His Calendar, His cyclical dwelling place, etc. that Unity is a foregone conclusion!

By way of reminder, these Living Stones (from Ebeni, אַבְנֵי, the root of which is H#68 אֶבֶן, itself from a root indicating to begin to build; has a gematria of 53, the same as galal, to roll away, to exile) Further, galal is also the root of the word for Redemption, H#1353, גְּאֻלָּה, geullah. These Stones are being awakened and brought to their specific place in the Body much like the Bones of Ezekiel's vision! There is apparently then, an inarguable link between these "Ebeni" and the future Redemption of Israel!

Again, so as not to appear just randomly citing numbers, let me prompt your memory regarding the number 53 that is the gematria of 'Gan' – גַּן, as in garden, *the place where both Exile and Redemption occur for the second time*! The first occasion, took place between Genesis 1:1 and 1:2. A fact argued as the "Gap Theory" by some, but most lack the evidence we've presented you from early on in this book. As we look closer at the Hebraic word for garden, Gan, the simple picture is that of the Hebrew letter Gimmel presenting the prophetic word picture of the lifted-up, first-born of the Nun – Seed!

This snapshot also helps explain the Alef prefix of eben, which indicates a future tense 'I Will' followed by the Bet-Noon root ben - son, making eben literally "I Will Son You"! This is the mystery of Redemption! From Genesis 3 forward Adam had the sin-nature working in him and thus, his seed could not redeem his race from its fallen state!

Therefore, YHVH had to insert HIS seed into the Adamic Body – His DNA – as His WORD - alone could regenerate the dead bones, much like the vision of Ezekiel bones! The carnal flesh has death working in it, thus, the SEED – WORD has to get into the DNA – of the spiritual BONES first, this changes the molecular, physiological structure of the flesh, else the death, disease just reoccurs! A BODY – TEMPLE without the WORD MADE FLESH DWELLING INSIDE IS FULL OF DEAD MEN'S BONES!

This is why understanding the temporary nature of the Wilderness Tabernacle and the fatal flaws of its animal sacrificial system is paramount to distinguishing the Genuine Messiah from the Anti-Messiah who will suborn the masses with his hypnotic religious trances, I mean, traditions!

This whole charade being played out now as we write has one purpose and it hasn't changed since the beginning – B'reshiyt – of creation: That purpose is to prevent Godly Seed produced in the image of YHVH from propagating the earth!

Hence, we see the way in which the Creator flaunts His plan in the face of the Enemy, in a completely satirical manner – and in what for traditionalists, has become an eternal enigma, where the simple, viable, life giving remedy is found only in the language of the Creator – Hebrew! We see this in such words as Eben, where the Alef represents the Man/Husband and the Bet the Woman/Wife: The natural result of combining the two is offspring or SEED – I.E. the Nun!

What we see here, as we look at exile-death and redemption-life depicted in the parallel of these bones in Eden (Adam and Eve) with those of Ezekiel 37, is a bird's-eye view of Genesis 1:1,2 where the Tohu V'bohu exile of the heavens and the earth and subsequent redemption of that initial creation is seen first occurring! It is no different now! The Pattern never changes! Yet, His ways are higher than our ways and His thoughts higher than our thoughts? Could it be that we simply don't spend enough time getting to know Him and His Mind? Ouch…

We are presently in the midst of that same Tohu V'bohu – Exile – DARKNESS IS NOW UPON THE FACE OF THE DEEP, The deep being a future euphemism for man who has lost his garment of Light covering his body. The Ruach is now moving – H#7363, רחף, rachaph, to hover, vibrate, flutter or move upon the face of the Waters. A euphemism seen in the formed body or bones of the waters, being symbolic of People in preparation for the breath of

Ezekiel's Wheel Within A Wheel

the Ruach! Dear Reader, this is Redemption's final Prophetic Stage!

Take care, there's a curious twist seen here in the gematria of rachaph – 308 – the same as H#954, בוש, buwsh, a word seen first in Genesis 2: 25 and translated as shame, confusion, etc. It actually pictures a husbandman who is deprived of hope and harvest!

Further it is the root of an intriguing word seen in the discourse in Malachi 2:14 -16 dealing with how a Husband deals treacherously with his Wife – H#3830, לבוש, lebuwsh! The word for treacherous is bagad, to act fraudulently but has the same letters as begged – garment! Incidentally, lebuwsh has a value of 328, the same as H#2822, חשך, Darkness! From this we can ascertain that Adam acted treacherously with Chavah covering her with a bagad – a fraudulent garment of fig leaves! This symbolized a Covering for their Body or Tabernacle, which now, no longer had LIGHT or WORD or MESSIAH in it! We must be careful here, else the 3rd Temple campaign - whose adherents will not welcome Yahshua much less His Stranger Brothers from the dispersed of the remnants of Israel - find us in a בוש, buwsh, shameful condition where we are bereft of hope and harvest!

Before moving on, let's examine the above word rachaph that seems to be part of the inherent Character or Nature of the Ruach. The root stem – Resh – Chet, forms multiple words indicating to expand, spread out. Even found in such words as Rechem – womb or racham – compassion that indicates to 'spread out' as in, the bowels of compassion, to expand!

The Final Pey of rachaph, pictures the Mouth, to speak or vocalize! Thus, the Ruach's primary function is to expand, enhance, and spread out, to womb with compassion the SPOKEN WORD OF YHVH! No wonder the Bones of Ezekiel require the Ruach to breathe upon them! He is a husbandman whom the enemy thought to deprive of hope and harvest; to make ashamed yet, He now comes to REDEEM HIS EXILED BRIDE!

The gematria of the above phrase Tohu V'bohu also gives a bit of a clue: 430 is also the value of נפש, Nephesh, rendered as: breath, to take a breath – i.e. to rest, be refreshed.

Similar to the Resh-Chet roots, the original meaning of the root stem 'Pey-Shin' is also to 'spring about', to increase, be spread or scattered! The Nun prefix of course, hints at the SEED of LIFE – which is none other than the BREATH OR WORD OF YHVH – which, when planted into what seems an empty, lifeless form redeems, rejuvenates, refreshes, causes it to Spring About, be increased.

These words are not simply a fortuitous 'luck of the draw' by the author of Genesis! He took dictation at the tongue of the King of Creation's using His chosen dialect! No other language has the DNA changing power found in this 'Tongue of Men and Angels' – Hebrew!

The same Pey-Shin root hints at expunging or obliterating something, to strip off, unclothe, and remove ones garments! Strip off, as in the Fig Leaves, those fraudulent fleshly ones!

These bones contain the DNA – the SEED scattered to the 4-winds, yet still containing the identity of their Father!

Now, pay attention: This gematria of Tohu V'Bohu - 430 is seen a total of 8 times (8 is the number of Life, new beginnings) in the first 2 chapters of Creation – Genesis 1and 2: First, here in Tohu V'bohu; And in vs. 24 in the phrase - ויחיתו, vechaiyihto – *'and the Living Things' (beasts)* - of the erets-earth, and finally, 6 other times as 'Nephesh' with the last occurrence, one seen as a designation of the Purpose of the ADAM: Genesis 2:7,19. Why is this important?

Once YHVH breathed into the Adam (vs. 7) he BECAME a

"Nephesh Chayah"! Like YHVH Himself, he literally had/has the ability to breathe into; to cause to spring about, to increase (birth) to expunge or obliterate LIFE! *(The Last Adam said this: Thy Kingdom come. Thy will be done in earth as it is in heaven?)* Adam's purpose was to speak to the Exiles – in their Tohu V'bohu situation and cause them to be redeemed! He looked with hope toward a harvest!

**Note the similarities to the Mission of Yahshua!

Luke 4:18,19:

> The **Spirit-Ruach** of the Lord is **upon** me, because he hath anointed me to preach the gospel to the poor; he hath sent me to heal the brokenhearted, to preach deliverance to the captives, and recovering of sight to the blind, to set at liberty them that are bruised, To preach the acceptable year of the Lord.

Pay Attention to The Pattern Here!

After creating Adam and imbuing him with power, YHVH then formed the rest of the Living Creatures – *HE DID NOT BREATHE INTO or ON THEM* – but, having instead formed them, He brought them before the ADAM TO SEE – H#7200, ראה, ra'ah, to observe, cause to be shown, to approve, from Ro'eh – a Seer or prophet - what ADAM would breathe into or CALL – H#7121, קרא, qara', to proclaim, to summon, name, appoint, commission – to READ THE TORAH – them! Isn't this a powerful, hidden revelation that surely has the ability to shake us to the core while exciting us to action? Hallelujah!

**Note Acts 1:8:

> You shall receive power after the Ruach HaKodesh is come upon you…

Could this happen to these bones as well? If so, where is OUR POWER?

The key word above is 'call' - Qara – and has a value of 301, the same as Alef-Shin, אש, Esh, translated as fire. Adam called and released the FIRE of YHVH into the animals! Esh can also mean 'THERE IS ONE! Is there one? This is the root of both Ish – Man and Ishah – Woman! Ish – Man; a word, which is not seen until the Ishah – Woman, is created. He truly was a husbandman expecting a harvest! Are you Dear Reader?

Moreover, this word Esh - Ish hints at the sexual relationship between man and woman: The original Creational Edenic Purpose of Adam and the Woman regarding Intercourse was nothing more, nor less than: The ability to speak and cause to 'Spring About', to increase, to produce *or to expunge or obliterate life*! To declare: THERE IS ONE! I SEE IT! The Breath of YHVH is meant to release SEED into the WOMB! This is Faith! YHVH did not release His Breath into the Animals; neither did the Adam until Genesis 3. However, in like manner He allowed the Adam to speak to or over them! It was after the fall that Adam took on the BEAST nature and released seed into the flesh of the woman! It is this beastly nature that is in EXILE and in need of REDEMPTION!

Following the pattern of speaking life into existence, that same LIVING TORAH –WORD – Eternally known as: The Messiah - echoes the question posed to Ezekiel: "Son of Man, can these bones live?" Remember this is what Ezekiel is then told in response in chapter 37:4:

> *Again he said unto me, Prophesy upon these bones, and say unto them, O ye dry bones, hear the word of the LORD.*

Notice the TRANSITION! Ezekiel is told to Prophesy UPON the Bones, not into them, thus bypassing the BEAST – FLESH nature! If he speaks to the beast nature, the flesh first, then the same thing that killed them originally will kill them again! The Spirit of Man must be renewed and that changes the flesh! This is the basic premise of the entirety of the Vision of Ezekiel and the Wheel Within a Wheel! There is a threshold between the Spiritual and Physical realms a place where only the Righteous may enter! Yahshua bridged that chasm thereby, restoring your ability Dear Reader – by Faith – to speak to the Dry bones in your own life! Most hesitate thinking there is some sort of responsibility on our part! Yet, take note what follows!

There's an explosively, powerful revelation that most have never seen in this interesting word used here: Prophesy, H#5012, נבא, nava', translated here as *the ability to speak by inspiration as moved by another's power and not one's own.*

Thus, causing something to germinate, sprout or burst forth! NOTICE it has the same letters as EBEN – I WILL SON YOU! From banah to begin to build – Could this speak of the foundational Stone – the DNA – from which all others are formed?

Genuine Prophesy will release SEED UPON the SPIRIT MAN causing something to burst forth, spring up, and be released! Sadly, most "prophesy" comes from the animal spirit, the flesh of the person and is based on emotion or known issues and is often birthed out of PRIDE – A WANTING TO BE SEEN! It produces nothing, TICKLING THE BEAST while exacerbating the EXILE OF THE HEARER! Anyone prophesying without dynamic faith results should be openly questioned.

Prophecy doesn't speak from the flesh to the flesh: I.E. emotions, that which is already known, or seen in the flesh! It speaks to the SPIRIT MAN calling those things, which are NOT as though they WERE! This redeems the flesh, setting it free, causing it to live! YHVH will not release His Seed into the beastly nature! Why should we attempt to?

This is the purpose of the RUACH breathing upon the Bones of Redemption - to build a Tabernacle not made with hands – Hebrews 9:11 a Living Stones Tabernacle! We can prophesy to the DEAD BONES – DEAD STONES all we want but this will never produce the Unification of the Whole House of Israel spoken of in Ezekiel 37!

Without the DNA of YHVH the Tabernacle of Adam-Chavah lacked the LIGHT: Darkness reigned upon the face of the deep - until the Light was restored! John 3:19:

> *And this is the condemnation, that light is come into the world, and men loved darkness rather than light, because their deeds were evil.*

Sadly, at the time of Yahshua, the Pharisees were the party representing the religious views, practices and hopes of Israel, while the Sadducees were the priestly caste. Both groups represented the Temple common to Yahshua's day, yet He spurned them calling them Sepulchers instead – full of dead men's bones! Incidentally, there was NO ARK OF THE COVENANT TO BE FOUND WITHIN THAT TEMPLE! Further, there will be none in the 3rd Temple either! Who, where is that Ark of The Covenant? He is at the Right Hand of the Father!

Need I Make it Plainer?

The 3rd Temple's construction is a fleshly-beast natured creation; it DOES NOT REPRESENT THE BONES OF EZEKIEL'S VISION! Why? Joseph is not welcomed there and his kinsmen are those bones, further, he is a TYPE OF MESSIAH YAHSHUA – WHO ALSO IS NOT WELCOME! Contrarily, ABBA is speaking upon the Living Stones – The SPIRITUAL Bones of the House of Israel gathering them from the four corners of the Earth!

Ezekiel's Wheel Within A Wheel

Note the following: Ezekiel is told to prophesy – Nava - העצמות-על, al-h'etzmote – upon these bones? This is intriguing, because the preposition על, al, upon, on account of, to go up, to *spring up*, (Isn't this the same meaning as the root of Nephesh?) is also the root of another word meaning shame עלב alev, and it, alev, is the root of עלה, Eleh, meaning leaves, representing the beastly, fleshly garment Adam and Chavah *chose* to clothe themselves with! This book, and the visions of Ezekiel reveal that he was indeed - a husbandman expecting a harvest! He did reap what was sown!

The Round Tabernacle or Tent, and the substitution of Animal Sacrifice were a lower, corrupted illustration like Adam's flesh. In order for man to obtain his original incorruptible form they served as a physical reminder of the condition of the Flesh after the fall and the need for the Blood of the Kinsman Redeemer. By way of reminder, the Hebrew word for Tent is written H#168, אהל, ohel, translated as tent or covering but from ahal, meaning to be bright, to shine, to have a vibrating appearance!

It's also worth noting ohel's similarity - אהל - to the letters of Eleh – leaves: עלה, as in fig leaves which were Adam and Eve's covering of choice – for hiding their Beastly Nature. Eleh has a value of 105, while the value of ohel is 36 a difference of 69. This number is the value of H#5206, נידה, Niddah; a term indicating the menstrual cycle and is also a familiar term depicting an exilic period. Therefore, as we've mentioned hitherto in this work it's not an accident that the Niddah cycle is connected to the lunar gestational cycle, in particular the 3-dark days of the Moon! Light is about to break forth as the Ruach hovers over the darkness of the TENT!

It is highly possible that Adam and Chavah could have returned to the Tent of Ohel - Ahal – the place of Vibrating Light – אור, owr, but chose instead the Tent of skin – H #5785, עור! Now, you understand a little more why the Wilderness Tabernacle emphasized its skin coverings! This is almost blasphemous! How could Adam and Chavah have remained in the Edenic Tent? Because The Voice – DNA – came to speak to the BONES immediately in the cool – RUACH of the day! Hovering over the waste and desolation Tohu V'bohu, the darkness!

Remember this! The reintroduction of DEATH to the Body of Adam brought with it the hybridized Seed of the Nachash through the spiritual doorway into the natural realm – Genesis 3! As Adam and Chavah – Eve if there are consequences for eating, dwelling at the wrong Altar-Tabernacle? Did they really have a remedy, one already dispatched before the foundation of the World? Revelation 13:8?

The word for Voice in Hebrew is: H#6963, קול, Qowl, voice, a sound, to call aloud, but it can also indicate lightness and leniency! What? The Voice came offering leniency to the Adam and Chavah? How? Why? Perhaps the gematria will help: Qowl has a value of 136, the same as the phrase that establishes the law of reproduction in Gen. 1 'After It's Kind' – למינו, leminu!

As incredulous as it seems, it looks as if The Voice comes offering leniency in spite of the SIN OF ADAM and ISHAH. Is it possible that because of the Law of producing after one's kind, that an avenue still remained up to this point for their restoration - but instead, they hide themselves – not as a result of the sin, but because of their current naked condition?

HMMMM? Isn't this intriguing? While here pay attention to the related words for light and skin: their respective gematria: אור, light – 207, עור, skin – 276 a difference of 69 which again, connects us back to the value of that powerful and unique Hebrew word– Niddah- translated as unclean or Darkness-Exile!

It is also not a coincidence when we see Ezekiel being commanded to prophesy 'upon these bones' - al-h'etzmote – this specific grammatical term 'upon these' rather than 'to these' is not accidental making the value of the phrase 711 – which is also the value of another familiar Edenic phrase: ביום אכלך ממנו מות *B'yowm alkalekah mimehnu mote*: In the day that you eat you shall surely die! This is what happens when we speak to or from the BEASTLY FLESH nature or if we hear it, thus receiving or entertaining its seed, wombing it in our minds; it continues to die in Exile! Hence, we are admonished regarding the need to renew the Mind as shown in Romans 12:2:

> *And be not conformed to this world: but be ye transformed by the renewing of your mind, that ye may prove what is that good, and acceptable, and perfect, will of God.*

To add further scriptural collusion to our scheme, these Bones of Redemption have to be sown into the earth in order to reap a harvest called resurrection. Thus, Messiah was planted Himself in order that the Bones are enabled to become Redemption stones and by His resurrection, connect us to the concept of the Tabernacle of Lively Stones being formed in the fashion of a

Man, that Man who was none other than the High Priest after the order of Melchizedek who established a Priestly order comprised of those Redeemed Saints! 1Peter 2:5:

> *Ye also, as lively stones, are built up a spiritual house, an holy priesthood, to offer up spiritual sacrifices, acceptable to God by Messiah Yahshua.*

Likewise, His bones – Messiah, are prophetically comparable to the UNION of the *sticks of the 2-Houses of Judah and Joseph – Ephraim,* seen in Ezekiel's vision in chapters 37-39. Again, pointing us to a distinct pattern leading to both a Spiritual and Physical "UNITY". The Living Stones – Living Bones being divinely connected with the DNA of the Creator resonating within each!

Interestingly, that word for sticks is, H#6086, עץ, Etz, the singular form of Etzem – bones or trees. As in Ezekiel 37 the gathering of these stones or *'Bones of Redemption'* אַבְנֵי גְאֻלָּה, Ebeni geullah - a phrase with a gematria of 239 - connects us to another interesting phrase: וְעֵץ הַחַיִּים – v'etz h'Chaiyim - *And the Tree of Life (lives).* Adam and Chava were depicted as euphemistic trees established as living offshoots of the Righteous Branch and who, sadly because of sin were exiled from this Tree!

However, He made a way for us, in order to glorify YHVH as written in Isaiah 61:3b *that they might be called trees of righteousness, the planting of the LORD, that he might be glorified.*

It's also encouraging to note that these Bones of Redemption - Ebeni geullah could also be rendered stones or 'Bones of Exile'. The root being H#1540 גלה, galah, translated exile, but is a word that also hints at an uncovering, in other words; to be revealed, or to be made naked. This word hints at a Body, which is uncovered in a shameful fashion outside the parameters of designed intimacy – this leads to exile! Adam and Chavah are made naked and ashamed because the Light – Word – the Messiah no longer resides upon, within them! The Temple without Messiah is naked and ashamed!

This same word for uncovering, galah is likened to the ear being hidden until the hair is pulled back, or the face veiled and then the veil removed! This seemingly points to the Secret things revealed in the intimacy of Marriage chamber, which is usurped in an untimely, untoward fashion. Of course, the first instance of this is found occurring in Genesis 3 where the Bones of the House – Adam and Chavah – are made naked and the Way to Redemption revealed. Please remember that this WAY – Zodiac in fact means 'Way' – was established from Genesis 1:14 and is still a fixed way for us today!

We must also throw into the bargain, the text of Genesis 2:23

where Adam describes the Woman as: עָצֶם מעצמי ובשר מבשרי - etsem m'etsemi ubasar m'basari – translated as: Bone of my bones and flesh of my flesh. There can be no UNION OF THE HOUSE IN THE 3RD TEMPLE IF THE SOURCE OF THE DNA OF THE BONES IS NOT ALLOWED!

What I'm about to say may be offensive to some, but, geullah – galal can mean both Exile and Redemption. Thus, the same circumstance may be viewed as exile to some while redemption to others, thus, it is possible that how we see ourselves, be it through the eyes of victim or victor – may determine whether we stay exiled, cut off, or whether we're able to experience the exhilaration of being set free! Further, there seems to be a season of "Uncovering – Exposing" - a Galah - appointed for this entire group! This reveals the RIGHTEOUSNESS OF THE HOUSE! Only Exile does that! This heart attitude separates captive from Freeborn!

Redemption imputes the righteousness of the Melchizedek, The King of Righteousness, who is both High Priest and Kinsman Redeemer, as a result, His Standing, His inheritance, His abilities – are inscribed upon the tablets of the heart of those redeemed! We were unable alone to secure that redemption and animal sacrifice never had the means to do so by itself! This sobering concept forces one to change his current exiled mindset to that of the mind of the Kinsman Redeemer

He, who alone is able to demonstrate His Lawful Standing as the Foundational Corner Stone and if we are indeed Living Stones, we must abide in Him! It is certainly the season where the EAR IS BEING UNCOVERED! The Hebrew word for ear is, H#241, אזן, Ozen, the organ for hearing, it is often used to infer the receiver of divine revelation, yet when styled with different vowel points, it also indicates a sharp weapon for keeping the Camp of Israel clean so that the Presence of YHVH can walk among His People! The combined value of Ozen, and galah – Uncovered ear – is 96, the same as the phrase: ילד בן yalad ben, to bring forth a son!

The Living Stones Tabernacle – The Ohel Mo'ed – Tent of Appointed Times is the Intimate Place representing Gan Eden – The Garden of Appointed Times! Thus, if Messiah is not welcomed in the Tent – Garden – The Righteous Temple; there can be no doubt that another Genesis 3 incident is about to arise where, at a presumed season, divined from a false calendar, and instituted by a false priesthood who will sanction their own 'Proper Time' - a counterfeit bride, the scarlet and purple clad woman of Revelation 17:3,4 will - *yalad ben* – bring forth a son from the FALSE MESSIAH and we will continue to live manifesting through the beastly nature!

Is it a coincidence that the Anti-Messiah has the False Prophet and the BEAST as cohorts? One who speaks falsely to the Dead Bones all the while attempting to resurrect their Beastly System!

That being said, it seems at present, that the Believing community is conjoined with a mixed multitude that will be divided over the GATHERING OF THE BONES OF EXILE – REDEMPTION! A great disputation will occur over the recognition of these Bones or Lively Stones! A clamor such as never been seen or heard will thrust this Priestly Band into a position where their Unified Righteousness and Integrity will generate a miraculous power summoned in answer to the cries of the rest of creation whose earnest expectation has long awaited the Manifestation of these Sons of Elohiym!

All of the above seems to hint at a season of EXILE followed by the REDEMPTION of the House, which then prepares the way for its UNIFICATION! This seems to be the premise of the entire discourse of Ezekiel. His vision regarding the Wheel Within the Wheel, the Zodiacal 360-day Calendar, their correlation to the Tabernacle's Round construction all seem to fit into part of reclaiming what was lost during the Exile and what must happen in order to reveal the identity of the Remnant - THE BONES

WHO WILL STAND ON THEIR FEET AND LIVE! The last step is their Unification! Let's stop here for a second...

The Kinsman Redeemer and Your Redemption Rights

Torah is rife with reference to the role of the Kinsman Redeemer: One who alone must offer himself or provide other sufficient price for his near kin. Following that line of thought, it is my opinion that the Genesis 3 encounter took place at YOM KIPPURIM – THE DAY OF COVERINGS. Further I also contend that Joseph's brothers sold him into slavery on this same date:

**Note Jubilees 34:11-15:

> *And in the seventh year of this week he sent Yoseph to learn about the welfare of his brothers from his house to the land of Shechem, and he found them in the land of Dothan. And they dealt treacherously with him, and formed a plot against him to slay him, but changing their minds, they sold him to Ishmaelite merchants, and they brought him down into Egypt, and they sold him to Potiphar, the eunuch of Pharaoh, the chief of the cooks, priest of On. And the sons of Yaakov slaughtered a kid, and dipped the coat of Yoseph in the blood, and sent (it) to Yaakov their father on **the tenth of the seventh month**.*

For Joseph it may have seemed Exile, but he became the instrument of Redemption and His Seed – The Bones of Redemption are carried out of Egypt when the Exodus occurs. The Bones of Joseph Live and are about to obtain their INHERITANCE! עוד יוסף חי Od Yoseph Chai! Yes, Joseph is Alive and it is my contention that Ezekiel witnessed the prophetic design, the Eternal Plan of the Creator, to provide for his redemption at a dark time upon the earth, a season like no other. As he did in the Exodus pattern, Joseph will be tested.

The opportunity will be presented to compromise with the wife of Potiphar, H#6318, פוטיפר there is no consensus pertaining to the origin of this word. Though I believe it's a compound of two separate words or phrases: First, the Tet and the Tav are both Hebraic dental letters with phonetically similar sounds and are thus, interchangeable in translation. There is no viable Pey-Tet root, but there is Pey-Tav which is a contracted form of a root indicating the corner of the head, the forehead specifically. The latter letters, Yod-Pey-Resh seem to be a phrase where the root par, to bear fruit and the prefixed Yod – 3rd person qal imperfect: continuing action in the past or future: 'He was, is, and will be doing'. It seems a hidden reference to a past; present and future mark in the Forehead of those who compromise with this Counterfeit Harlot in the House!

There will be acute, contentious division in the Judeo-Christian-Messianic-Hebrew Roots community over the genuine Righteous Standards as well as, the Righteous King and True High

Priest of the House – Bride of YHVH! There will also be a clever, charismatic counterfeit: Anti-Messiah, a False Temple-House, and a False Harlot clothed in the colors of the True Tabernacle, scarlet and purple!

My Dear Reader! This book was written to aid you in your quest for truth. To enable you to see the depth of the deception that is the World-Wide Religious system embedded like a cancerous tumor within the head of the Judeo-Christian-Messianic-Hebrew Roots community! I want to call your attention to Jeremiah 29:11 one last time:

> *For I know the plans that I have for you, saith YHVH, plans of peace, and not of evil, to give you in your latter end a hope.*

Finally, I want to close these pages with my prayer for you. I have taken the privilege of author and I have added or deleted some words from the KJV for clarity's sake, inserting for transparency, what has been revealed to me through the personal trials that have birthed this book. I am solemnly convinced that it will not diminish the Word! It is taken from Colossians 1: 9-29:

> *For this cause we also, since the day we heard it, do not cease to pray for you, and to desire that you might be filled with the knowledge of his will in all wisdom and spiritual understanding; That you might walk worthy of Yahshua unto all pleasing, being fruitful in every good work, and increasing in the knowledge of YHVH; Strengthened with all might, according to his glorious power, unto all patience and longsuffering with joyfulness; Giving thanks unto the Father, which hath made us able to be partakers of the inheritance of the saints in light: Who hath delivered us from the power of darkness, and hath translated us into the kingdom of his dear Son: in whom we have redemption through his blood, even the forgiveness of sins: Who is the image of the invisible Elohiym, the firstborn of every creature: For by him were all things created, that are in heaven, and that are in earth, visible and invisible, whether they be Tabernacles, or thrones, or dominions, or principalities, or powers: all things were created by him, and for him: And he came before and he is before all things, he is their pattern and by him all things consist. And he is the head of the body, that Living Stones Tabernacle: he who is the beginning, the firstborn from the dead; that in all things he might have the preeminence. For it pleased the Father that in him should all fullness dwell; And, having made peace through the blood of his execution stake, by him to reconcile all things unto himself; by him, I say, whether they be things in earth, or things in heaven. And you, that were sometime alienated and enemies in your mind by wicked works, yet now hath he reconciled in the body of*

his flesh through death, to present you holy and unblameable and unreproveable in his sight: if ye continue in the faith - grounded and settled, and be not moved away from the hope of the gospel, which ye have heard, and which was preached to every creature which is under heaven; whereof I Paul am made a minister; Who now rejoice in my sufferings for you, and fill up that which is behind – summing up what has been written of old, their patterns; revealing that which was lacking in my flesh, your flesh, that I might accept the afflictions of Messiah in my flesh for his body's sake, which is the True Lively Stones Tabernacle: Whereof I am made a minister, according to the dispensation of Elohiym which is given to me for you, to fulfill the word of YHVH; Even the mystery which hath been hid from ages and from generations, but now is made manifest to his saints: to whom YHVH would make known what is the riches of the glory of this mystery among the Gentiles-The House of Joseph – who will form the final Tabernacle; which Mystery is this - Messiah Yahshua must be in you, He is the hope of glory: He Whom we preach, warning every man, and teaching every man in all wisdom; that we may present every man perfectly mature – Filling up the full stature that is Messiah Yahshua: Whereunto I also labor, striving according to his working, which worketh in me mightily.

May Abba Bless you and Keep you!

Amen!

www.ingramcontent.com/pod-product-compliance
Lightning Source LLC
Chambersburg PA
CBHW060349190426
43201CB00043B/1782